Free & Eazy Circles

Jan Mullen

Magic Ballz & Other Foundation Follies

C&T PUBLISHING

Text © 2006 Jan Mullen

Artwork © 2006 C&T Publishing, Inc.

Publisher: Amy Marson

Editorial Director: Gailen Runge

Acquisitions Editor: Jan Grigsby

Editor: Sara Kate MacFarland

Technical Editor: Gayl Gallagher

Copyeditor-Proofreader: Wordfirm Inc.

Cover Designer: Kristy Zacharias

Design Director/Book Designer: Rose Wright

Illustrator: John Heisch

Production Assistant: Tim Manibusan

Photography: Bewley Shaylor unless otherwise noted

Published by C&T Publishing, Inc., P.O. Box 1456, Lafayette, CA 94549

Front cover: Various circles by Jan Mullen

Back cover: *Looking for My Prince*, and *The Birdz and the Beez*,

by Jan Mullen

Library of Congress Cataloging-in-Publication Data

Mullen, Jan,
  Free & eazy circles : magic ballz & other foundation follies / Jan Mullen.
      p. cm.
  Includes index.
  ISBN-13: 978-1-57120-346-5 (paper trade)
  ISBN-10: 1-57120-346-X (paper trade)
  1. Patchwork--Patterns. 2. Patchwork quilts. 3. Circle in art. I. Title. II. Title: Fast and easy circles.

TT835.M8235 2006
746.46'041--dc22

2005036373

Printed in China
10 9 8 7 6 5 4 3 2 1

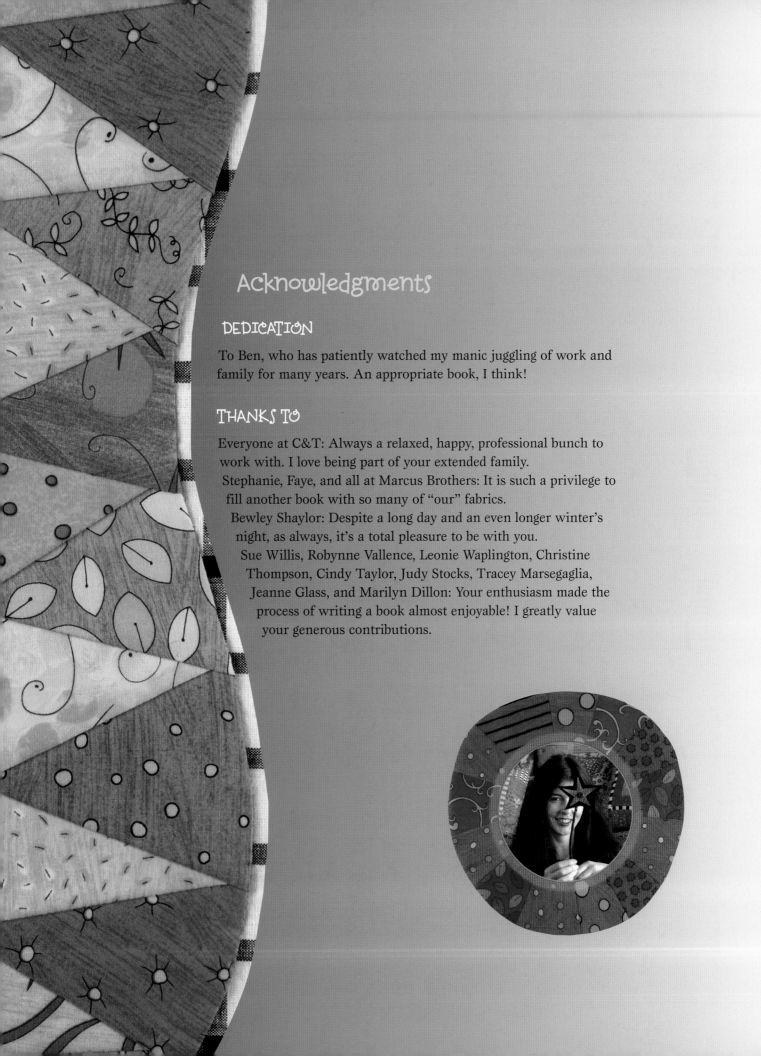

Acknowledgments

DEDICATION

To Ben, who has patiently watched my manic juggling of work and family for many years. An appropriate book, I think!

THANKS TO

Everyone at C&T: Always a relaxed, happy, professional bunch to work with. I love being part of your extended family.

Stephanie, Faye, and all at Marcus Brothers: It is such a privilege to fill another book with so many of "our" fabrics.

Bewley Shaylor: Despite a long day and an even longer winter's night, as always, it's a total pleasure to be with you.

Sue Willis, Robynne Vallence, Leonie Waplington, Christine Thompson, Cindy Taylor, Judy Stocks, Tracey Marsegaglia, Jeanne Glass, and Marilyn Dillon: Your enthusiasm made the process of writing a book almost enjoyable! I greatly value your generous contributions.

contents

Have a cuppa!

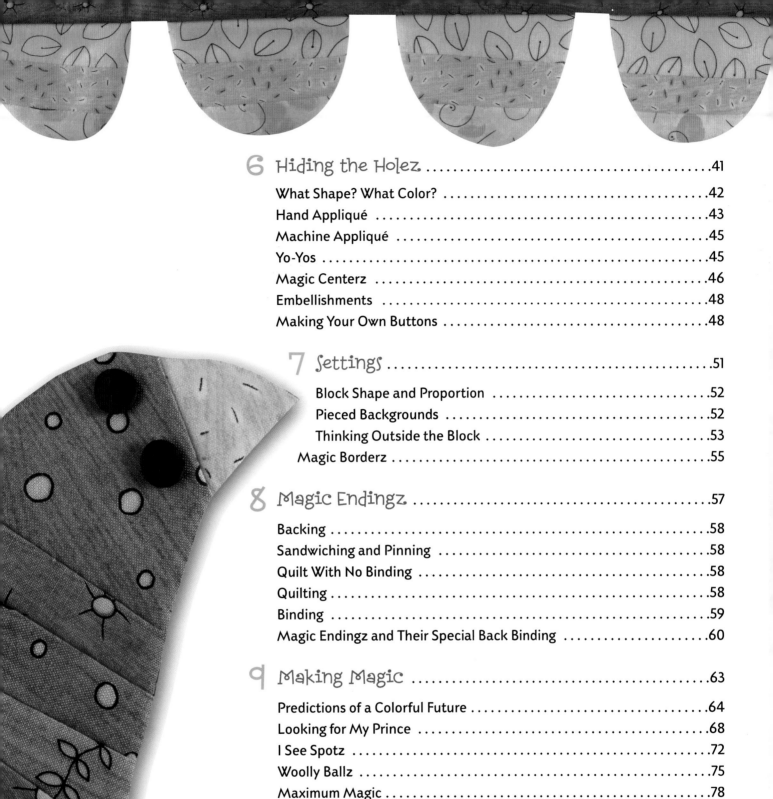

Introducing Magic Ballz

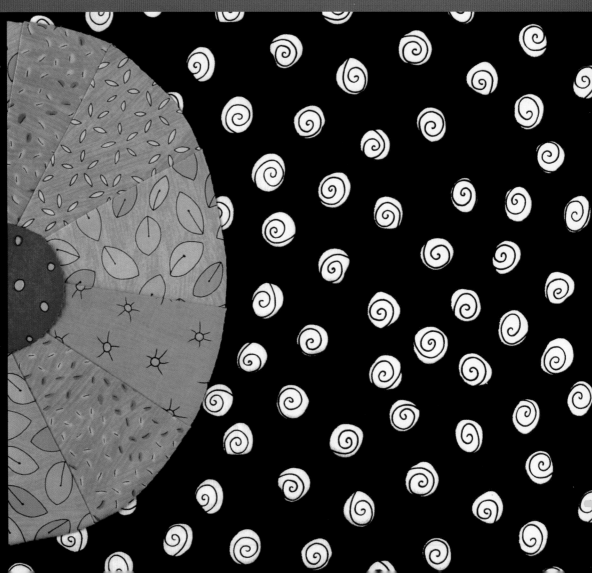

Funny name, Magic Ballz. Let's get the sly comments and jokes out in the open right away, and then we can get on with the serious business. Quite finished? Then, let's continue.

The processes in this book are easy to understand and execute, which means it's very easy for you to be creative—to play with design, color, and fabric.

Magic Ballz refers to a technique of piecing wedgez onto a circular foundation in a freeform manner: *Magic,* because working freehand takes the headache out of working with circles and perfect measurements; *Ballz,* because the wedgez covering the foundation remind me of a beach ball. I also think Magic Ballz sounds better than Magic Circlez. But with all the sniggers, I am not so sure!

The original Magic Ballz block started as a contemporary extension of the traditional, and often intimidating, Dresden Plate block. As usual, in my hands, it has morphed a long way from there. Early on, I made four versions, in between producing more traditional pieced quilts. Each had only small changes, with the main differences involving their colorways. Magic Ballz #3 went into pattern format for the world to make and has continued to be a quiet favorite ever since. When I rewrote and updated the pattern in 2001, I added a list of ways to change the ballz and blocks; my usual brainstorming tendencies were kicking in. Essentially this book refines and fleshes out these ideas.

What's special about the method? It's easy and not at all intimidating!

Appliquéing by hand is easier than usual with this method. The turned edges rarely require clipping, for three reasons. First, breaking the ballz into wedgez eliminates tedious clipping because the stitching stops at the edge of the foundation, essentially leaving a clipped edge. Second, the foundation, if it is batting, creates a small soft ridge that reduces the severity of turning edges, making stitching easier and less likely to be jagged. Finally, freehand cutting and piecing of the foundation eliminates the precision usually required. An unintended by-product is that working on a precut foundation also makes it easy to fill space.

The processes in this book are easy to understand and execute, which means it's very easy for you to be creative—to play with design, color, and fabric. Magic Ballz blocks often become springboards to executing designs whose initial source isn't easily identifiable.

How best to approach this springboard then? A quick read through the chapters will soon have your ideas bouncing:

Chapter 2 introduces the equipment and techniques needed to make the ballz.

Chapter 3 runs through the basic process of making a Magic Ballz block.

Chapter 4 shows many ways to change the wedgez.

Chapter 5 has options for finishing the edges and attaching the ballz.

Chapter 6 explores ways to cover the holez.

Chapter 7 covers settings for Magic Ballz blocks.

Chapter 8 offers alternate ways to finish your quilt.

Chapter 9 is full of projects that will reinforce and add to what has been covered in the preceding chapters.

And sprinkled throughout are some wonderful works by some enthuziastic students.

Let the bad punz begin ...

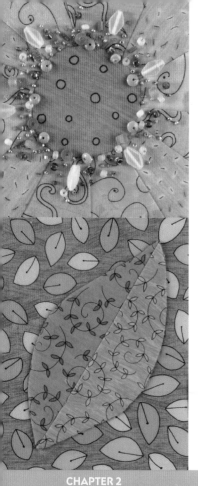

Essential Equipment and Techniques

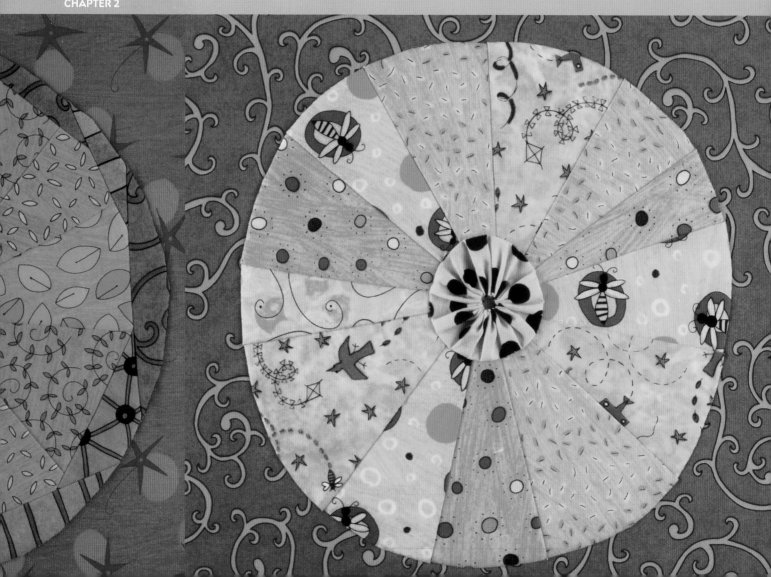

CHAPTER 2

BASIC EQUIPMENT

CUTTING EQUIPMENT

Rotary cutting equipment. Although this is not essential, it certainly makes wedge cutting and piecing easier. The sizes of these tools should relate to the size of your work. Bigger is definitely better, so if your block is to be cut 12½″ × 12½″, you should invest in a ruler of that size rather than just using the mat measurements.

Scissors. You can use scissors instead of a rotary cutter, but take care to sew the wedgez with a straight seam. You may like to trim the outer edge with scissors, although I am partial to the speed and smoothness of freehand rotary cutting. Either way, be sure to have some sharp fabric scissors on hand. Paper scissors, of course, are the only type to use if your foundation is paper.

Thread clippers. This tool is wonderful for trimming threads and tiny pieces of excess wedgez. I simply couldn't work without my clippers. Have a pair by the sewing machine, the iron, the TV, you name it!

Unpicker? Of course you won't need one, but having it handy may be advisable.

SEWING EQUIPMENT

Sewing machine. Although you can make basic Magic Ballz using the simplest straight-stitch machine, the newer machines do have wonderful features to increase the quality, speed, and pleasure of your work. I regularly use the needle up/needle down feature and the knee lift; they make life easy when making magic. A variety of programmed stitches may be useful, too.

Specialized feet. These are essential. A walking foot is used every time batting is involved in the stitching process, so it is a good idea to invest in one. Without it, you will get drag as the top piece of fabric pushes forward. I use a ¼″ patchwork foot for general piecing. A quilting foot or darning foot is also essential if you are freehand quilting, stitching, or couching.

Pins. Invest in a variety of pins, buying the best quality possible. Appliqué pins make preparing hand appliqué easy. Choose pins with a large head, either glass or plastic, to make their placement easier. Use medium-length pins for general piecing, quilter's pins for pinning the edges of the sandwich together, and small safety pins for pinning the quilt sandwich.

Needles. You'll need these for hand appliqué and finishing the binding. Special appliqué needles, with their fine eye and sharp point, are best. A large needle chosen because it is easier to thread will puncture your fabric and may fray delicate edges. A visit to your optometrist may help!

Thimble. If you use thimbles, I don't need to extol their virtues. If you haven't used them, then learn to—it will improve your stitches and save your skin.

Iron. Steam is good. Iron after every seam to make the crooked grain of the wedgez and the ballz lie flat. Use it also to shrink the batting as you work.

Marking equipment. I keep a regular pencil, a silver pencil, and a sharpener handy for use on fabric, as well as a chalk wheel for marking temporary stitching or quilting lines. There are many types of markers available. Use what suits you.

Quick sketches for foundation shapes

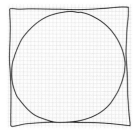

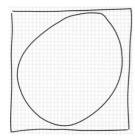

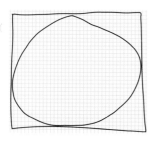

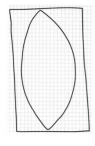

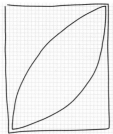

THE FOUNDATION

You have choices for the foundation, depending on the way you prefer to work.

Cotton batting. I use a needle-punched cotton batting as my "normal" foundation. This material is firm to work on but not stiff. It withstands ironing without melting. It has a gently filled look and gives a lovely edge to hand appliqué. The batting may shrink, so press it along with the first seam.

Paper foundation. Use typing-weight paper, joining pieces with a glue stick if necessary. (I use the UHU glue stick.) Stitching should be smaller than usual (1.5 to 2) to allow the paper to be torn out easily. Start and stop stitching on the edge of the foundation with tiny stitches or backstitches. Paper's advantage is that the edges stay crisper, and the seam allowance of the wedgez can be pressed over. It doesn't add bulk to the quilt either. Iron the allowance to the back, using the paper to give the edge. Carefully tear off the paper. I fold each paper wedge open and score the seam with my finger-nail; it then tears easily and lifts out.

Lightweight foundation. Use this in Magic Edgez, Magic Centerz, and Magic Endingz to add a little fill and dimension. It also serves as a good foundation for stitching curves and points. I prefer Pellon's lightweight foundation.

Other foundations. Interfacings of various types may be used, but they would not be removed as other foundations can be. Many are too stiff or too soft. Fusible interfacing is problematic as a foundation; avoid using it.

I have not included templates in this book; instead there are loads of quick sketches and ideas to give you basic shapes. I love the look of freehand work and encourage you to incorporate a personal style to your work—with my help, of course!

I have included rectangular measurements as a parameter for you to cut ballz and other smaller shapes. You'll waste a little batting, but the speed and ease of working this way wins, hands down.

WEDGEZ

Fabric. I use cotton to make most of my quilts. The possibilities are endless and are constantly changing, with fresh designs continuously available. Consider the play of color and the scale and proportion of the prints, as well as the mood it will invoke. I gently prewash my fabrics and have them pressed and ready to use.

Other types of fabric may also be used. Using a foundation makes working on slippery fabrics so much easier. Recycled ties would work well in this technique. You may also consider using linen and looser or thicker weave fabrics.

Cutting the wedgez. A rotary cutter gives you a straight edge to sew against, and the Magic Ballz stay flatter as a result. Cut individual wedgez from scraps or cut multiples from stacked strips. Grain is not important, because the foundation and the walking foot eliminate a lot of the drag. See page 22 to help estimate the size you need to cut.

Cutting individual wedgez. From scraps, use a straight edge on at least one side.

Cutting wedgez from strips. Use the desired height of the wedge. You determine the length.

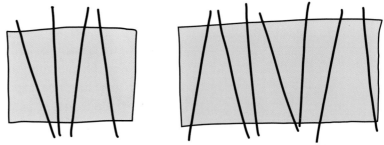

Stack cut strips. A maximum of four fabrics is usually plenty. The strips can be of different sizes. You may want to start by cutting a minimum number of wedgez, pinning the stack, and cutting more as needed.

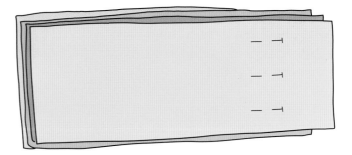

Consider the play of color and the scale of the prints...

THE "ISH" FACTOR

You will see measurements here with the suffix "-ish." This is to remind you that this measurement does not need to be perfect. *Ish* means a little bigger, a little smaller, a little crooked, or perfectly sized—all will work. With this freeform style, we celebrate difference. Ah, if life were always like this...

PIECING

WEDGEZ

When using cotton batting as your foundation, use a normal stitch. Secure the outer edge with backstitches or small stitches, if you feel the need. The inner edge can be left unsecured, because it will be covered.

A perfect 1/4″ seam is usually used in patchwork, but we only need to do that if we are setting blocks in a traditional fashion. If you are not a 1/4″ master, use the edge of the presser foot as your guide. I happily do a bigger or smaller seam if it helps achieve the look I'm chasing.

Use the top wedge as your guideline for a straight seam. You can trim excess fabric on the lower wedge after you sew the seam.

Chain piecing. Chain piecing, a method of piecing many patchwork sections without breaking the thread in between, can't easily be employed here. I still use a pile of foundations and work through it almost as efficiently, but I have to trim the threads each time.

Pressing. I press after every seam I stitch. I press every wedge as I go. The grain needs to be kept under control. Despite the interruption of the stitching, pressing makes the work flatter and crisper. Don't be lazy here!

Use a quarter-inch foot or patchwork foot and a traditional 1/4″ seam when joining blocks. In general, it is easy to join blocks in rows and then join the rows. If you plan your pressing, you can alternate seam direction and butt the seams to make matching points easier.

HAND APPLIQUÉ

I love hand appliqué. It is something I love to do at night while relaxing in front of the television. Like most appliqué devotees, I work the basic technique to suit my own style and comfort. I like to work on a stable base, usually a tray or a table, so that I can pin and keep the tension in check. Most of the ballz in this book were hand appliquéd. I like the process, but even more, I like the look of it—soft-edged and filled. Many of the centers were hand appliquéd too. No centers were marked; instead they were cut freehand.

The stitch should be close to invisible. Choose a thread the same color as the top fabric, veering toward a darker rather than a lighter one. Start with a knot at the back of the ball, the center, or the background, and bring your needle through the fold.

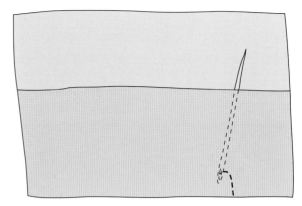

Make the first stitch by placing the needle in the background, behind where the needle came up. Angle the needle so that it goes behind the fold.

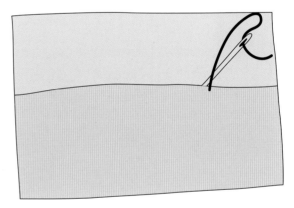

Take the needle across the back of the background and up again through the fold, this time a stitch length, maximum of 1/4″, from the first. Your stitches should be almost invisible.

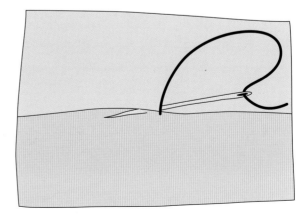

Continue on in this manner. Points and valleys may need a couple of extra stitches to secure them.

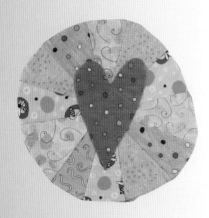

All set now?
Let's go!

CHAPTER 3

The Basic Magic Ballz Process

First things first: All new processes should first be tested by making a sample block before leaping headlong into a project.

Right here, right now is the perfect place and time to understand the Magic Ballz process...

All new processes should be tested by making a sample block before leaping headlong into a project. We all know this, yet many of us cut copious amounts of fabric before we have a proper understanding of techniques or how they suit us. Right here, right now is the perfect place and time to understand the Magic Ballz process, to iron out any problems, and to gather thoughts about what you would like to do with these ballz. No procrastination or bluffing is allowed. Grab a "cuppa" (tea, coffee—your choice), gather your materials, and spend a wee while stitching.

I'll first lead you step-by-step through making a "normal" Magic Ballz block. The samples and projects in this book are all merely variations of this first block. We'll postpone the variations and projects until later.

MAKING A "NORMAL" MAGIC BALLZ BLOCK

MATERIALS

Batting: 10″ × 10″-ish square of stabilized cotton
Assorted coordinating fabrics: 6 squares 6″ × 6″-ish for wedgez
Background: 12½″ × 12½″ square
Center fabric: 3″ × 3″-ish square
Rotary cutter, board, and ruler
Sewing thread to coordinate with your wedgez fabric
Sewing machine with a walking foot
Scissors
Appliqué needle and thimble

PROCESS

1. Freehand cut a circle from the batting; crooked is good.

2. Cut a center hole with the diameter approximately 1½″. Off-center is fine, too.

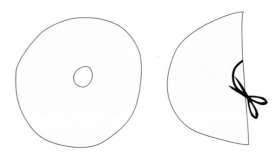

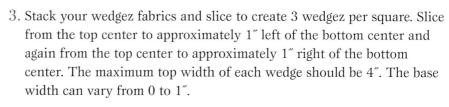

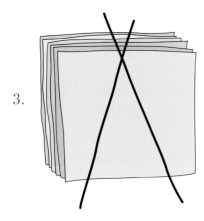

3.

3. Stack your wedgez fabrics and slice to create 3 wedgez per square. Slice from the top center to approximately 1˝ left of the bottom center and again from the top center to approximately 1˝ right of the bottom center. The maximum top width of each wedge should be 4˝. The base width can vary from 0 to 1˝.

4. Place 2 wedgez on the foundation, right sides together and right edges aligned. Pin. If you aren't using a walking foot, use 2 pins across the seamline to hold. Leave *at least* 1/4˝ of fabric overhanging the outer edge. Starting from the outer edge, machine stitch down to the hole. Backstitch or use tiny stitches at the end. Don't stitch the overhang, otherwise you may have to clip it later. Open the wedgez and press. I also press the foundation at this stage to eliminate shrinkage.

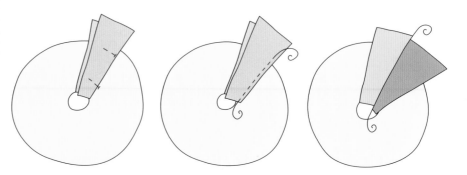

5.

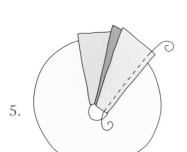

5. Working clockwise, place a new wedge right side down on the right-most wedge. Using the new wedge's edge as the seam guide, place the wedge so that the seam runs from the outer edge of the foundation to the center of the hole. Pin, if necessary, and leave *at least* 1/4˝ of fabric overhanging the outer edge. Machine stitch from the outer edge of the foundation to the hole as before and backstitch. The wedge underneath may need to be trimmed to bring it level with the new wedge. Open the wedge and press.

6. Continue until the foundation is almost covered with wedgez. You may work in both directions when space allows. Always aim the stitching line from the outer edge to the center. Trim any unnecessary bulk from beneath new wedgez and trim excess fabric in the center hole to keep it clear. The final wedge needs to be quite large to enable an easy closure. It should overlap the first wedge by at least 1˝.

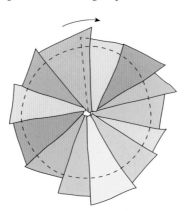

7. To close the ball, you have 2 choices:

Hand appliqué. If you hand appliqué the ball to the background, simply fold under the raw edge of the final wedge and pin. When you are ready to stitch the ball to the background, begin your stitching near the center of the ball and finish off the last wedge before you begin stitching the ball to the background.

Machine closure. If you prefer an instant closure or if you will be machine appliquéing the edge, the process involves more stitching and trimming:

1. Place the ball right side up on the cutting mat.

2. Bring the edges of the first and last wedgez together midair, forming a center seamline. Push the edges to the left and make a crease; this will be the final seamline. Use a small ruler to carefully slice the foundation at the edge of this seamline.

3. Place the ball right side down, with the opening slice at the top. Pull the right edge of the slice toward you, exposing the overhang of the first wedge. Use the ruler's 1/4″ line to measure a new wedge edge 1/4″ out from the cut foundation. Slice.

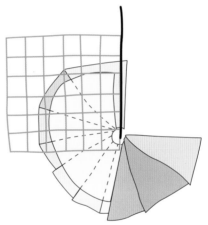

4. Turn the ball, still right side down, so the opening slice is at the bottom. Pull the right edge of the slice away from you, exposing the overhang of the final wedge. Use the ruler's 1/4″ line to measure a new wedge edge 1/4″ out from the cut foundation. Slice.

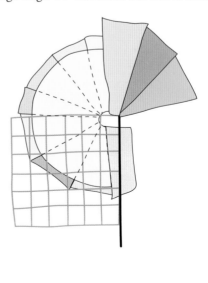

5. Place the ball right side down, with the opening slice at the top. Use the ruler's 1/4″ line to measure a new edge 1/4″ out from the cut foundation. Slice.

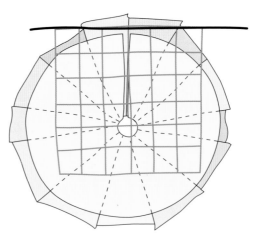

6. Place the first and final wedgez right sides together, with recently trimmed raw edges, top, and side aligned. Stitch the seam along the edge of the foundation.

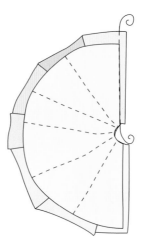

7. With scissors or a rotary cutter, trim the overhang to 1/4″-ish from the edge of the foundation.

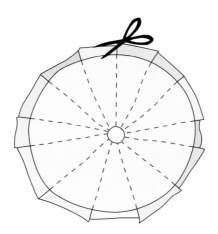

8. Place the ball on the background. Pin the raw edges under the foundation as you pin it to the background. Pin from the outside in to help push the edges under. Appliqué by hand. See page 35 for stitch basics. If your preference is to machine stitch, see page 34 for other ideas.

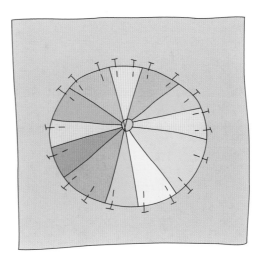

You may now trim the excess background fabric away from the back of the ball, although I rarely bother to do this.

9. Cut a freehand circle from the center fabric, making sure it will cover the hole. Appliqué by hand.

That is enough for you to get started!

I hope you aren't lying curled up in a ball of angst. If you are OK, read on for a multitude of inspirational changes—though it's probably time for a fresh cuppa, first!

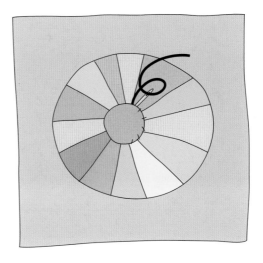

Looking Into the Magic Ballz

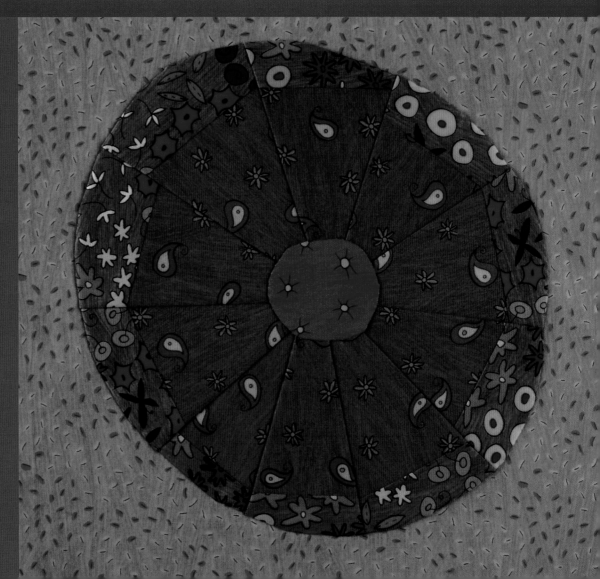

You've made a sample block and now you want to explore. In this chapter, we look at changes we can make to the wedgez and the foundation.

Unless otherwise stated, the sample blocks in this chapter are the "normal" Magic Ballz introduced in Chapter 3. Backgrounds were cut 12½˝ x 12½˝, the foundation of batting was 10˝ x 10˝-ish before shaping, the wedgez were cut from 6˝ strips, and the edge and simple circle centers were appliquéd by hand.

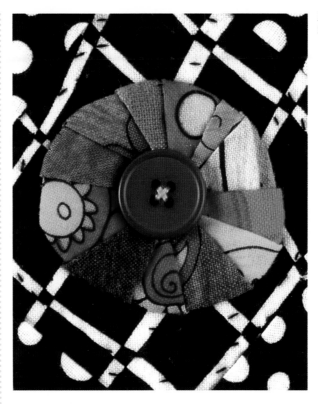

Little Magic Ballz, Jan Mullen,
$2^{1/2}'' \times 3^{1/2}''$, 2004

I haven't made a gigantic one yet, but in theory, a solo Magic Ball could be made to sit atop a king-size bed.

BALLZ SIZE

Any size is possible, but the logistics of making either teeny or gigantic ballz have to be thought through. The smallest one I have made is on an artist trading card. The ball was only 2″ across and was hand stitched onto the batting foundation, with a button to cover the hole. Very sweet and surprisingly quite pleasant to do.

Imagine using old ties this way! Those luscious old fabrics would find a fabulous new use. The slippery fabrics would be easy to sew. It would be a stunning guy's quilt.

Will someone make one please and send me the photo?

WEDGEZ SIZE

What size should the wedgez be? What size *could* they be? With the "normal" Magic Ballz block, the size to cut the strips and then the wedgez was given. But how do you estimate height and width of a wedge when you want to change the size of the ballz?

Wedge height. The height of each wedge depends on the size of the foundation. Measure from the center of the hole to the edge of the foundation and add an inch for the overhang. For example, the normal Magic Ballz block was cut from a 10˝ square—half of this is 5˝ and the added inch makes 6˝.

Wedge width. The width of each wedge depends on the look you seek. The samples that follow illustrate some of many possible options:

Constant size. The width at the top of the wedgez were cut 4˝-ish and the bases anywhere from 0 to 1˝-ish. If you want calm and regularity, this is the way to go.

Irregular size. The wedge top widths varied from 4˝-ish to 2˝-ish and the bases from 0 to 1˝-ish. This still looks ordered but is probably more interesting than the previous sample. It also makes it easier to hide the final wedge, which might otherwise be a different size.

When the hole is not central. This hole was cut about halfway between the edge and the center of the foundation. The longest wedgez were 7˝-ish and the shortest only 4˝-ish. If the wedge top width is constant, the longer wedgez will have the illusion of leanness. To counteract this, make the long wedgez wider than the short wedgez.

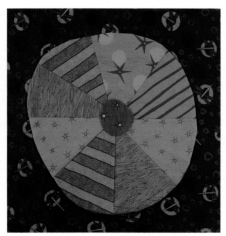

How big? The widths of the tops of these wedgez were 5˝-ish, and the bases were from 0 to 1˝. Bigger tops can be good, because fewer wedgez means less stitching. The downside is the lack of ease in appliquéing a sweet curve—there is still no need to clip, but only just. If the wedge tops are cut wider than 5˝, clipping the outer edge may be necessary. Achieving a good color balance also becomes more difficult with bigger and fewer wedgez.

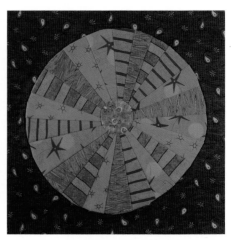

How small? I could have gone smaller here than the top width of 2˝-ish and base of 0, but there seemed to be little reason. This was enough stitching! I did discover though that very little wedge trimming was needed here—the 0 base was perfect.

USE OF COLOR

Color is a very personal thing. Color use projects different emotions and incites different responses. Keeping the psychology and personal taste aside, let's look at using color's most basic qualities.

High contrast. Many of my early Magic Ballz quilts had wedgez low in contrast and often monochromatic. This helped concentrate attention on the shape of the ballz and the shape in the center. When the contrast in alternating wedgez is high, the block becomes rather graphic and confronting.

High contrast wedgez of different sizes. The proportion of the alternating wedgez changes color dominance—the blue is now the dominant color, despite being recessive. The shards of orange are still the focus, though. The blue wedgez are "normal" (top width 4″, bases 0–1″), and the orange wedgez are cut "skinny" (top width 2″, base 0).

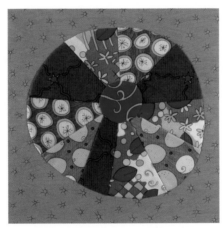

Spokes. I played what-if here: Could I insert strips not wedgez? Yes, I could, and the result is reminiscent of bike wheels. Again I kept the contrast high to show variation in size and shape. The blue wedgez are "normal" (top width 4″, bases 0–1″), and the orange wedgez have morphed into perfect 1″ strips. When stitching these, be careful to aim the strips to the left center, or you may find they eventually point off-center.

Big print fabric. The design on any medium-sized print will often be lost when cut up. With a big wild print, however, that can be a very good thing! If you use all big prints, the ballz will be very busy and may lose the wedgez' definition. Calming the ballz with a quiet background is the usual thinking, but a wild print in a contrasting color would be … wild!

Scrap. I'm a fan of scrap anything—partly through thriftiness, partly through "green" leanings, partly just the challenge of using what I have. Mostly though, I like the visual overload of scraps, the antithesis of order. Unfortunately one block doesn't do the topic justice.

Robynne needed a quilt for a youngster. Her wedgez use all sorts of prints as a Magic Ballz eye spy quilt. Her ballz have a lovely sense of calm despite the scrap fabrics—perhaps because they are of regular size and shape. Maybe also because the appliquéd strips help fill the blocks and ground them nicely. Buttonhole stitch by machine makes it very serviceable.

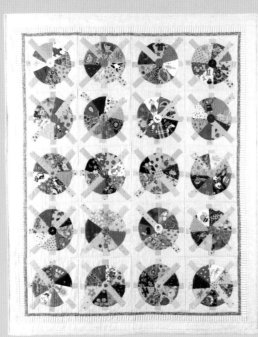

Sunshine, 46^1/$_2$″ × 66″, by Robynne Vallence, Western Australia, 2005

HOLLOW BALLZ

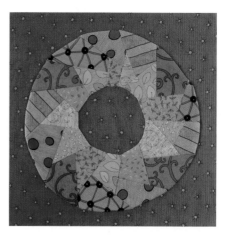

Hollow. Now the fun is really starting. I've replaced the ballz with ringz—half the piecing, double the appliqué. Here my wreath foundation was 2½″-ish wide, and the wedgez' heights were cut 4½″, adding an allowance of 1″ extra on both edges. With less angle needed on the wedgez, the top widths were 4″-ish, and the bases were 2″-ish.

Weaving around a ring. While experimenting with crazy piecing, I came up with a plaited effect. Replicating it around a ring was a bit trickier than I anticipated but worth the time and effort. It would also work for a "normal" Magic Ballz block. My coloring is subtle; with higher contrast, the "star" in the center could be accentuated. I struggled at first to get the angles correct but slowly developed a rhythm. To finish I stitched a partial seam on the outer edge and treated it like one wedge before appliquéing it closed. My wedgez were rectangles (2″ × 4″-ish) and needed to be well trimmed after each seam.

Cindy loves stars and decided to enclose them within her Magic Ballz. Her four blocks show to great effect the play on wedge size and number. Making them required skill, dedication, and time! Despite some pretty wide tops, she still had no need to clip the overhang.

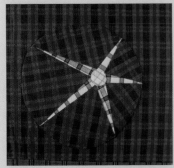

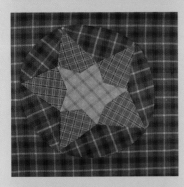

Four Stars, each 13″ × 13″, by Cindy Taylor, Western Australia, 2005

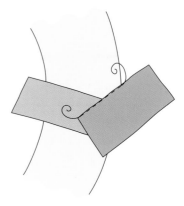

Starting the plait

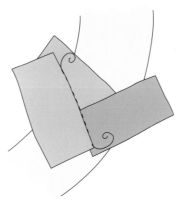
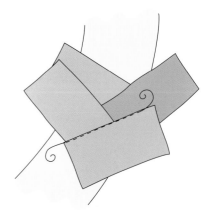

Continuing the plait

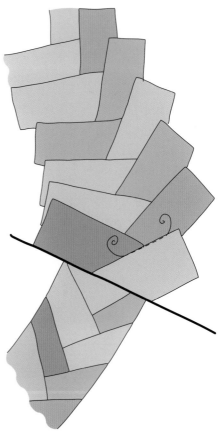

Finishing the plait

Wedgez with edges. Stitching on normal wedgez and later adding a log cabin edge has the potential to change the look dramatically. Here I pieced the wedgez and trimmed them to foundation size. With strips of contrasting fabric placed log-cabin style around the edge, I created an orange peel border. The appliqué is a bit more difficult, as clipping may be needed. This technique is useful as a patching device if your wedgez are too short.

PREPIECED WEDGEZ

If you start prepiecing your wedgez fabric, or even the wedgez themselves, the options become limitless. This does involve more cutting and stitching, but the effects can be stunning.

Two-tone strips. Strips can be divided in any proportion. Here I have replicated the look of the previous sample, but the ease of prepiecing suited me better.

A two-tone strip will give wedgez with two different outer edges.

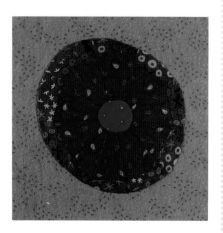

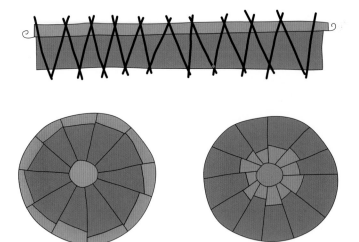

Piecing a three-piece strip with the same edges and discarding only the point of each wedge will give you consistent ballz. For the solo ball, my prepieced strip was made up of smaller strips 2″, 2″-ish, and 4″. The pieced strip, 24″ in length, made enough wedgez to cover the foundation.

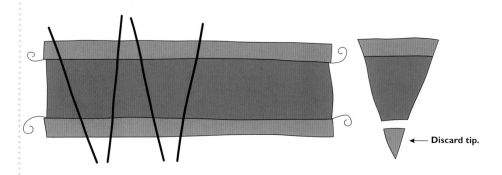

← Discard tip.

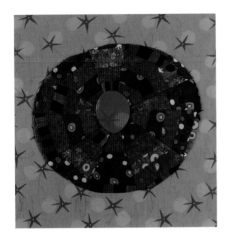

Strip wedgez. This version looks very intricate but was simply cut from a prepieced strip of 1″-ish pieces. The strips formed disjointed rings, subtle here in monochromatic fabrics. The more strip fabrics you have to work with, the more variety you will gain.

Cutting or piecing the "fabric" in a different direction will yield entirely different results.

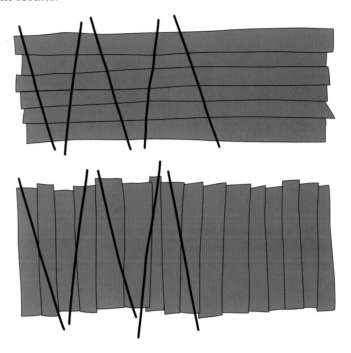

Another quilt from Robynne. This time her Magic Ballz become daisies with strips of green stalk and leaves. My Stargazey Quilts pattern Daisiez, used as an infill block, helped reinforce the theme. Her occasional use of pieced two-tone strips in some of the Magic Ballz adds complexity. This quilt was machine appliquéd using a buttonhole stitch.

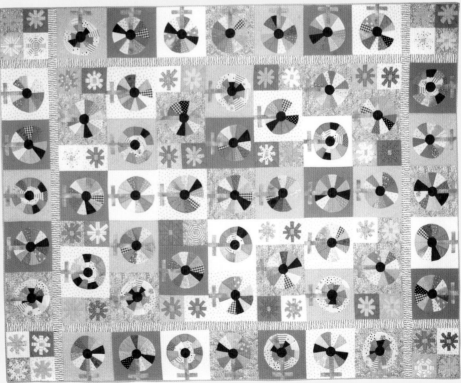

Michaelmas Daisy, 86½″ × 109½″, by Robynne Vallence, machine quilted by Sharon McGill, Western Australia, 2005

You've seen Cindy's star blocks, so it will come as no surprise that this clever lady also chose to play around with two-tone strips. Where my versions aim for free and easy, hers are feats of technical excellence that start from the loose space I encourage students to occupy. *Vive la différence!*

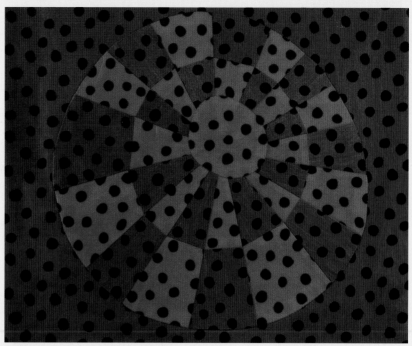

Double Trouble, 15″ × 15″, by Cindy Taylor, Western Australia, 2005

Alternate piecing. Need more interest in your wedgez? Why not alternate normal wedgez with pieced wedgez, either simple or complex? Lifesavers anyone?

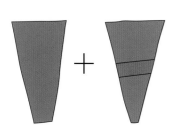

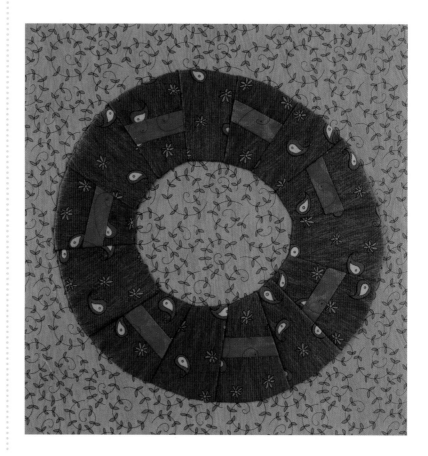

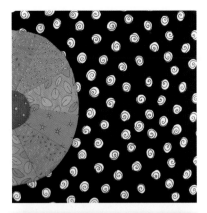

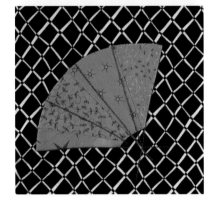

SLICING BALLZ

Magic Ballz can be dissected in many ways. They can be sliced as a foundation, as a pieced ball, or as a complete block. My usual piecing style is quite relaxed, and I use a lot of crooked slicing techniques. In the first sample is a ball sliced in half then appliquéd to a block. This would make a great border or a very graphic detail to repeat in the body of a quilt.

Next is a four-patch block made from two complete Magic Ballz blocks sliced in half vertically, then horizontally, and then restitched. The result—two smaller mixed Magic Ballz with a disjointed perimeter. The center was then stitched on and the block edges trimmed.

Finally, a third of a foundation was cut after piecing and then appliquéd to represent a fan. The sides of the foundation were trimmed back so the wedgez would cover the edges. Backstitched lines, using three strands of embroidery floss, enhance the fan image.

SHAPED WEDGEZ EDGES

Thinking of changing the ballz to another shape? What about pointy edges or petal edges? The principle should be much the same; it's a matter of simply piecing wedgez on a circle or preshaped foundation. The appliqué may be more difficult, as clipping seams becomes a distinct probability.

Working from a normal circle foundation but leaving the wedge overhang large and shapeable works. When I did this test run, however, I felt bogged down in technique—it wasn't as much fun as it should be. Where the seams joined, I had to resolve exactly where the shaping started. I decided I would only use this large overhang technique to shape the edges if they were to be left raw.

I used a batting foundation, leaving an indent that was itching to be accentuated. Again, backstitches with three strands of embroidery floss decorated the block. They sat just past the edge of the foundation and also accentuated the center. Use a paper foundation if you prefer the ball to lie flat.

I used this technique in the wool project on page 75 but sensibly left the edges raw.

Sue had the desire for shaped edges but came up with a different method of execution. Her lightweight batting foundation was covered by wedgez then simply cut into, batting and all, to shape where she needed. Appliquéing freehand by machine, couching luscious cords along some seamlines, plus extensive freehand quilting and embroidery, gave Sue a stunning result. The bonus for me is being able to show off her different approach.

Universal Fire, 46″ × 52″, by Sue Willis, Western Australia, 2005

Just when I've said that shaped edges are best left raw, up pops a sample to change my mind. Jeanne's interpretation of easy pointy edges was quite simple really. Why didn't I think of it? Place two wedgez of fabric right sides together. Stitch and trim the outer edges to a point before turning it right sides out. Then pretend these are "normal" wedgez on a normal foundation. Ingenious!

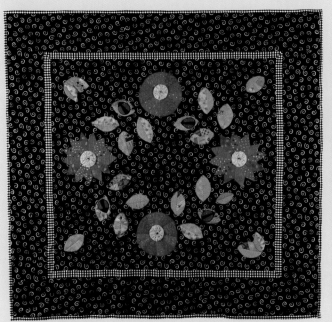

Magic Ring-a-Round, 63″ × 67″, by Jeanne Glass, Western Australia, 2005

NOT A BALL AT ALL

Let's lose the circle and cut some simple stylized shapes that are easy to cover and appliqué. This opens up design options, big time.

Keep in mind that wedgez aren't necessarily the way to work here. Strips or large lumps of fabric become much more useful.

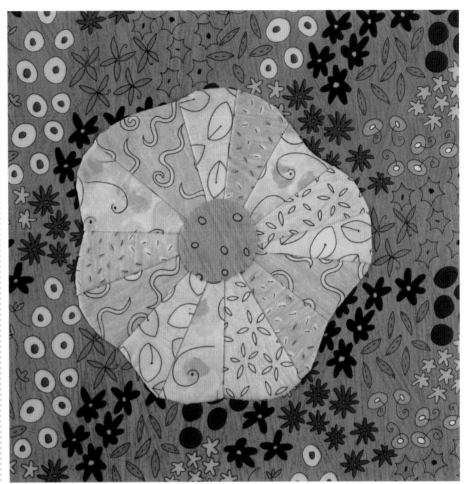

Carrot. Simple strips about 1½˝-ish wide are placed horizontally on the carrot and vertically on the stalk. I want to do the whole veggie garden now! Don't you?

Flower. This is merely a wobbly-edged Magic Ballz block. Wedgez were cut a bit smaller to give more detail.

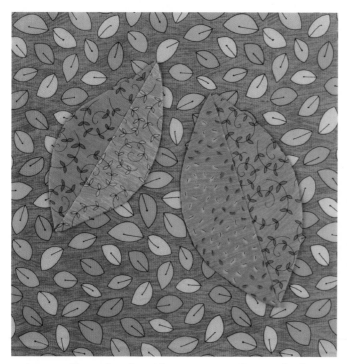

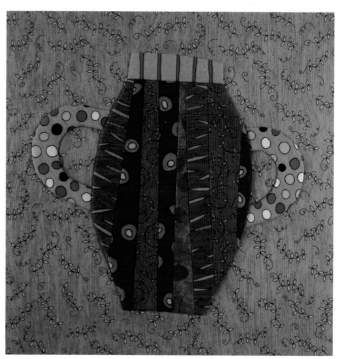

Leavez. Kept simple with two rectangles per leaf and one seam up the middle, these simple leavez are used in a few of the projects. Sometimes, for ease of appliqué, I place the seam off-center.

Urn. Vertical 1″-ish strips are covered at the top by a horizontal rectangle. The handles are appliquéd over a separate foundation.

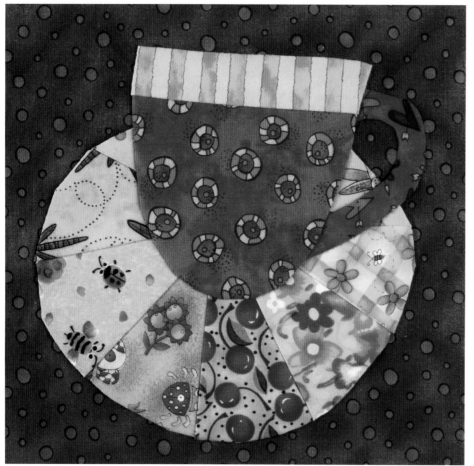

Cup and saucer. I love this one. It is a combo block—an incomplete off-center Magic Ballz saucer, topped with a shaped-foundation cup that is sized to cover the hole. The handle was also cut from foundation and covered.

Your cuppa should be finished by now. Choc-a-block full of caffeine, you're a ball of energy. Start stitching or read on . . .

Attaching the Magic Ballz

You've learned to stitch the wedgez to the foundation. Now you need to stitch them to the background. I usually choose to hand stitch the ballz to the background. However, although I enjoy the process of hand stitching and love the filled look it gives these blocks, it is not always suitable. Is there a way other than the "normal" hand appliqué? Let us look first at machine work.

APPLIQUÉ BY MACHINE

Machine stitching gives strength and is quite quick to execute, but it can flatten the ballz. If you are going to turn under the edges, machine stitching makes it more difficult to maintain a fine edge and a sweet curve. Edges can be pinned, pressed, or glued to hold in place. The most common stitch for machine appliqué is a small overlock or a zigzag stitch. Invisible thread is often used, but I'm not a fan; I like working with fiber.

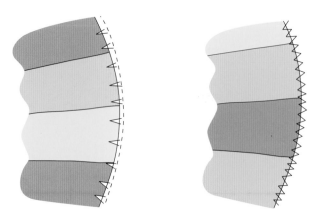

Using raw edges suits machine stitches and makes the ballz quick and easy to produce. Stitches can be bold or subtle. Below I have used a button-hole and a wispier stitch, both perfect for kids' beds.

DECORATING BY HAND

When using decorative stitches rather than invisible hand appliqué, I find it necessary to stitch under the edges first. This can be done by hand or machine. It is double the work but worth the effort. I used three strands of embroidery floss in each sample of buttonhole, fly, stab, and cross stitch, as well as some small center details of running stitch to tie in the look of the bold stitches. For another use of these stitches, see *Woolly Ballz* (page 75).

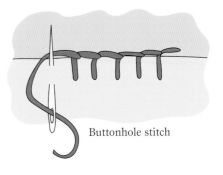

Buttonhole stitch

Fly stitch

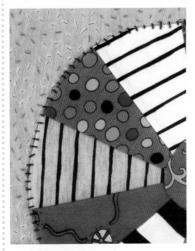

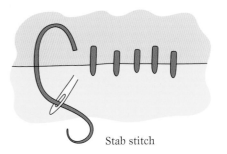

Stab stitch

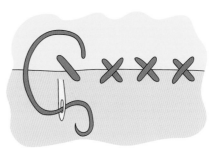

Cross stitch

EDGING WITH A TRIM

Bias binding. This lovely, defined, sturdy, easy edge uses commercial binding: Trim the wedgez level with the foundation. Pin the binding to the edge of the ball, with raw edges aligned and with the starting end folded back. Stitch on the fold. Press to the back. Pin to the background and stitch in-the-ditch of the binding to both secure and appliqué.

Fused bias. This fusible binding is even easier: Trim the wedgez 1/8˝ past the foundation. Place the ball on the background. Peel off the paper backing and carefully press the binding in position, covering both the edge and the background. Stitch along each edge of the binding.

Fully covered rickrack. I used a large rickrack here to easily cover the edge. Trim the wedgez level with the foundation. Pin the ball to the background. Cover the raw edge with rickrack and stitch along each edge. Freehand stitching is easiest.

Half-covered rickrack. Here I used the same large rickrack, but in a different way: Trim the wedgez 1/4˝ from the foundation. Stitch the rickrack through its center, 1/4˝ from the ballz edge. Press the raw edge to the back; half the rickrack will disappear. Pin the ball to the background and stitch in-the-ditch of the rickrack to both secure and appliqué.

Rickrack and little girls—don't they go hand in hand? Made for young Emily's bed, not only are these Magic Ballz sweetly colored and whimsically styled, but the rickrack also announces that a little charmer will lie beneath them. Machine appliquéing on a basic machine didn't hold Christine back at all—she's made excellent use of what stitches she had available.

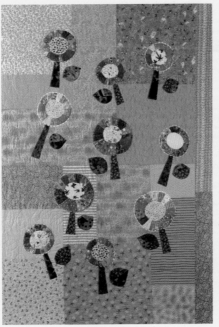

Daisy Dreaming, 55½" × 75", by Christine Thompson, Western Australia, 2005

Couching on thick threads. Trim the wedgez ⅛" past the foundation. Place the ball on the background. Stitch around the edge ⅛" from the edge to baste. In this sample, a hefty chenille thread was used to outline the ball then couched with a large zigzag stitch.

Pom-pom trim. I love this look, but the bulk of the trim did cause problems. I glued the trim to the edge and then hand appliquéd the ball to the background. For a similar use, see the flannel decorator pillow project (page 92).

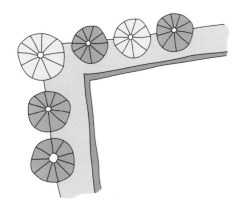

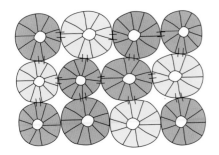

BACKING THE BALLZ

Another alternate edging is enclosed machine stitching, which is simply achieved by completely backing the ballz.

How to? After closing the Magic Ballz, don't trim the edges. Instead, place the ball right side down on some interfacing, lining fabric, or coordinating patchwork fabric. Pin and stitch along the edge of the foundation on the fabrics only. Trim the edges to 1/4″. You may be able to turn the ball right side out through the hole. If not, cut a small cross in the backing and turn through this. Depending on how the ballz are to be used, you may or may not have to close the back. An easy way to close the back is to tuck a small piece of fusible web inside the cross and press to fuse closed.

There are many ways to use these backed ballz: As free-floating semi-circles hanging off the edges of a quilt. As large substitute yo-yos loosely stitched together on or off a background. Or stitched on a background with a loose or sparse stitching design that doesn't use the edge at all. For the Magic Edgez that follow, having a backed ball makes for easy finishing.

MAGIC EDGEZ

If you want to move on from the simple circle without resorting to commercial trims, consider adding texture and design interest with some simple pointy or round Magic Edgez.

Pointy for suns. These were cut from strips of sandwiches 3″ wide and 24″-ish long.

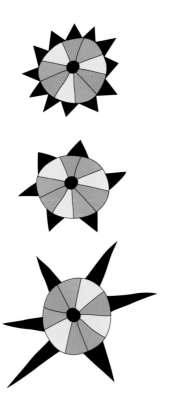

Round petals. These were also cut from strips of sandwiches 3″ wide and about 24″ long.

Three-dimensional sandwiches are simple to make. Two pieces of fabric are placed right sides together on a very lightweight batting. Shapes are marked, pinned, stitched, trimmed closely, turned, pressed, and then stitched under the edge of the ball. A slightly smaller stitch than usual will help when turning through and poking out any points.

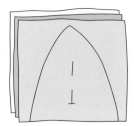

Pin the sandwich and mark the stitching line.

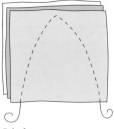

Stitch.

Trim ¹/₈″ from the stitching and trim points close.

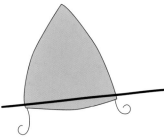

Turn, press, and trim the raw edges lightly.

Magic Edgez can be made individually, in pairs, or in groups.

A pair gives double the return with less effort than making two singles. Stitch the sandwich, leaving no opening. After trimming close, slice the sandwich in half before turning. If your slice is off-center, there will be more variety in your edgez.

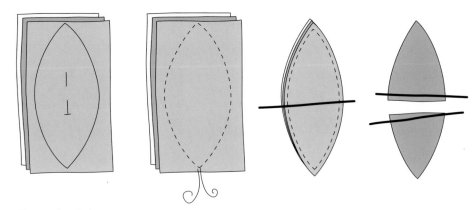

Pin, mark, stitch, and split before turning right sides out.

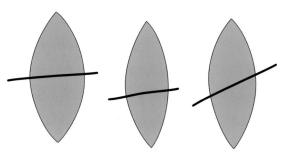

Slicing with variety

A group is an economical way to make many. Mark a strip sandwich with the shapes, perhaps "topping and tailing" only ¹/₄″ apart. Stitch down one edge on the seamlines and in between close to the raw edges before breaking the thread and stitching the other edge in the same manner.

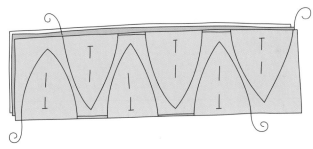

Topping and tailing: an economical grouping with a ¹/₄″ gap between shapes

Hiding the Holez

The samples so far have mostly had simple hand appliqué circles covering the holez. We'll take it further here, making the center covering more of a focus.

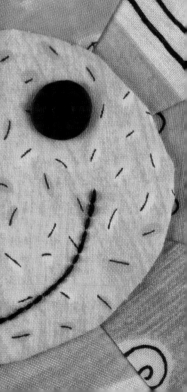

Any shape can cover the hole—hexagons, squares, wiggles, curls, stars, flowers.

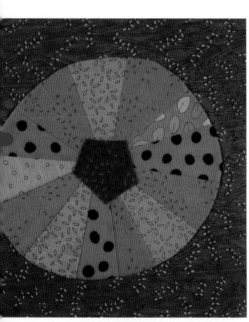

WHAT SHAPE? WHAT COLOR?

Circles are the obvious choice for hole coverings. These circles have to be big enough to cover the hole and be proportioned to enhance the ball. A circle cut from a 3˝ × 3˝ square usually works well, but it can also be bigger or smaller to change the look. If the center covering looks best large, you may choose to start with a large hole or merely use shorter wedgez.

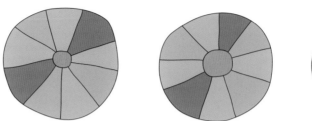

Use your imagination when you think about the hole coverings. If it can be cut out or stitched on by any means, it is an option.

Choice of color and fabric is the next concern. If the center is the same as or similar to the wedgez, it will blend in. If it contrasts with the wedgez, it should stand out. If it is the same as the background, it makes the ball look hollow, which is a great way to make an intricately inner-edged ball.

A more detailed visual can be obtained by repeating a shape. Here I managed to blend the black center with the blue wedgez by linking with a purple outer circle. This sample also suggests how a large print can be the focus: I picked out a daisy that ties in with the background fabric.

This darling little quilt has petite centers to suit the scale of the piece. Leonie has cleverly filled them with batting and used the double center trick to give focus. Little touches can add so much.

The Planet, Moon, and Stars, 18″ × 18¹/₂″, by Leonie Waplington, Western Australia, 2005

HAND APPLIQUÉ

When appliquéing by hand, raw edges are usually turned under. This seam allowance can be a bit tiresome, so the various cut shapes tend to be quite simple. When stitching centers lately, I have dispensed with the common ¹/₄″ seam and the clipping and notching that seam necessitated. Now I freehand cut the shape with a smidgeon of a seam allowance.

Here's how:

1. Cut the shape a tiny touch bigger than you need.

2. Sparsely pin the piece in place.

3. Thread a needle with a knot in the thread. Folding the seam allowance with your left hand as you go, or perhaps adjusting with fingers from both hands, stitch the edge, using the appliqué stitch (pages 12–13). Continue folding, holding, and stitching until complete.

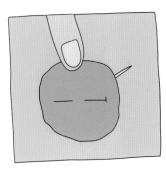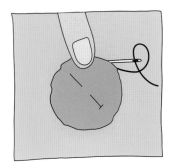

The immediacy of this method suits me. It relies on cutting skills instead of sewing skills; and because the cuts are freeform with a tiny seam, the method works well for anyone with strong visual skills.

Curves—both innies and outies—and points need separate consideration. Even with a tiny seam allowance, you may need to clip innies, notch outies, and slice off points.

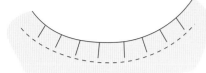

Clip innies.

Notch outies.

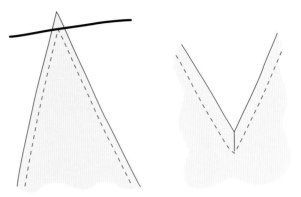

Slice off points and clip innie points.

Now you can do hearts and stars with ease.

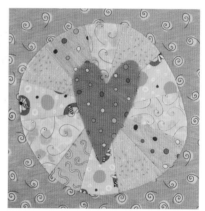

Next is the option of different threads and stitches to decorate. What works for decorating the ball also works well here.

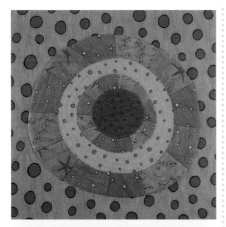

MACHINE APPLIQUÉ

For fancy shapes or for speed, machine appliqué is your answer. Hand-in-hand is the use of fusible web to adhere the shape without pesky pins.

The method is simple: Cut your fabric in a simple shape larger than you need. Cut a piece of fusible web slightly smaller. Fuse the web to the back of your fabric. Draw your shape, *in reverse*, on the paper and cut through all layers. Peel off the paper and press, with web side down, to adhere in position on your ball.

I keep sizable pieces—fat eighths and fat quarters—of an assortment of fused fabrics at the ready for this task.

Stitch with buttonhole, satin, zigzag, freehand, or any stitch you choose.

Use a multitude of shapes or layer shapes.

YO-YOS

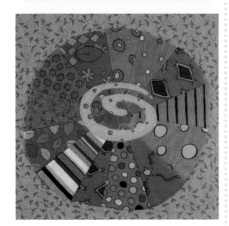

I love making yo-yos. I love the look of them. They add dimension and a bit of whimsy. Traditional methods dictate use of a perfect circle as your template—double the required circle size plus a smidge for the seam. But I find freeform-cut circles much quicker and easier. They team well with freeform-cut Magic Ballz, with their slight crookedness. See them used in *Maximum Magic* (page 78) and *Yellow Bloomz* (page 81).

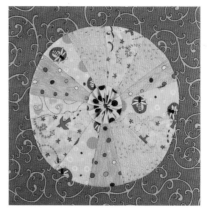

Construction is simple: Thread a needle and make a knot at the end. Folding the seam allowance as you go, stitch this down using a running stitch and gathering as necessary. The stitch length will determine how tight the closure will be—little stitches equal big hole, big stitches equal little hole. Finishing the circle is the hardest part. I stitch backward and forward through the gather a few times to tighten the hole before securing the thread.

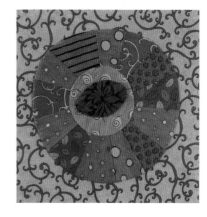

I have also experimented with freehand cutting other shapes too—ovals, squares, and triangles. Any shape can be cut, but a rounded-off shape works best. The same formula for size applies to other shapes—turn the edges under 1/4″ and stitch with single thread and a running stitch.

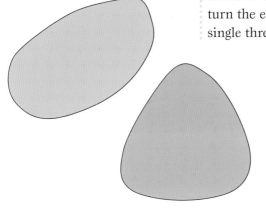

Speaking of yo-yos, the eye-catcher on Tracey's wall quilt is a group of bright red cherries—yo-yo variety, of course. Working on her tablescape involved finding the best resolution for her vision. The platter is without a center because a hollow edge gave a more realistic dimension. The strip-covered cupcakes have partial Magic Ballz on top, although the dribbles of rickrack icing are covering them. The tablecloth fringing needed to be attached realistically but without too much effort, so it is partially a quilt with no binding (page 58) with a bound piece of wall-hanging above. Empty picture frames are made in Magic Ballz style as a fitting finishing touch.

Pretty As, 32″ × 37″, by Tracey Marsegaglia, Western Australia, 2005

MAGIC CENTERZ

If we can have Magic Edgez on Magic Ballz, then we can continue the process and have pieces of magic covering the holez. Magic Centerz—three-dimensional whimsies—work the same way in that they create a great focus. Keep the shapes simple to avoid having to clip the seams.

1. Create a sandwich of lightweight batting, top and bottom fabric right sides together, and lightly pin. Mark the shape on the back of the top. Stitch on the line.

2. Trim the seam to 1/8″, clipping the seams in the valleys where necessary.

3. Cut a cross in the back and turn the sandwich right sides out.

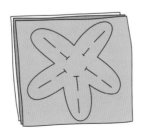

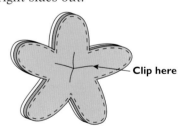

Clip here

4. Press. Close the hole by inserting a small piece of fusible web between the batting and the backing and press closed.

Shapes that work well include the straight-petal daisy, which has five clipped valleys.

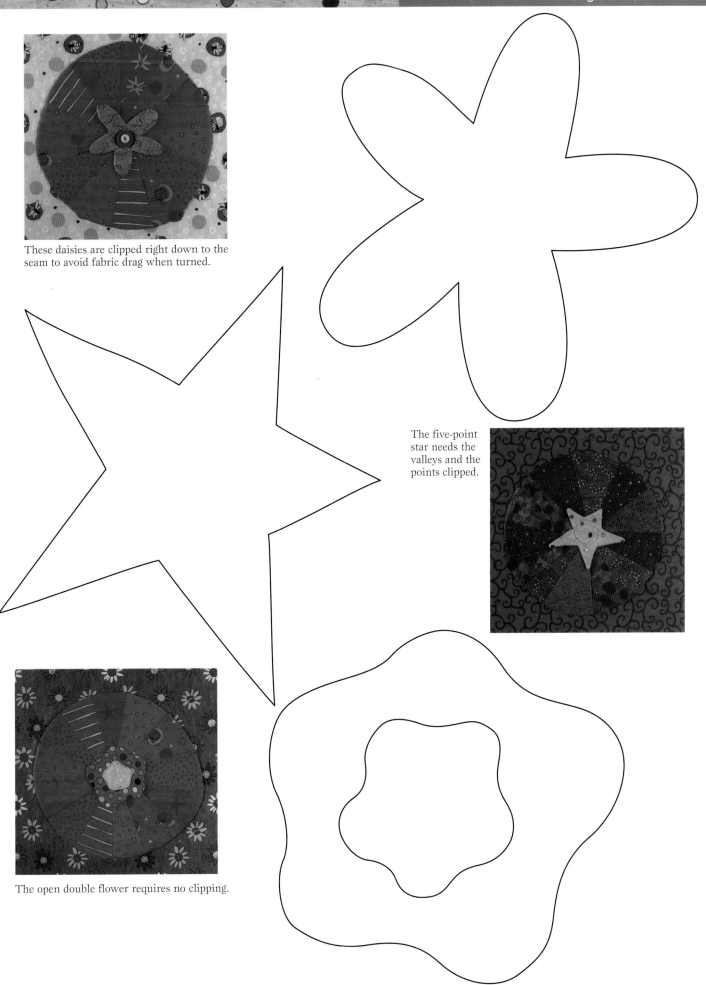

These daisies are clipped right down to the seam to avoid fabric drag when turned.

The five-point star needs the valleys and the points clipped.

The open double flower requires no clipping.

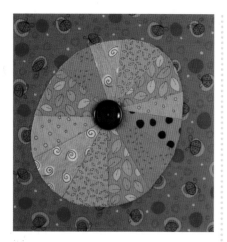

EMBELLISHMENTS

Buttons are an easy embellishment option. They create a real focus and can introduce dimension, extra color, and a change in texture. For a normal Magic Ball, though, the hole will usually be bigger than most buttons.

Exceptions exist, but you may find it easier to cover the hole with a similar or contrasting fabric and then stitch on your focus button. Here I made a mini Magic Ball, with the batting cut from a 3½″ square and the wedgez from a 2½″ strip with top width 1½″ and base 0.

Stitching a ring of buttons or a spray of beads is an elegant alternative. I scattered a mixed packet of beads and stitched them round and round in descending size until it looked balanced.

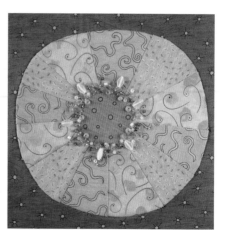

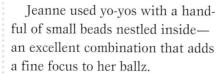

Jeanne used yo-yos with a handful of small beads nestled inside— an excellent combination that adds a fine focus to her ballz.

MAKING YOUR OWN BUTTONS

Lately, when I need a specific button color, size, or shape, I make my own from polymer clay. Fast and easy to make, these buttons have saved me from many frustrated shopping missions. Their lack of uniformity suits the carefree nature of my work.

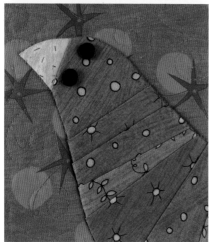

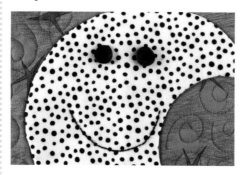

In my decorator pillow set on page 89, the moon and bird have pairs of tiny black eyes, while the bee has pairs of double-button eyes. These soft-rimmed round buttons are my favorite to make. They also look lovely. Make them fine and fussy or big and bold.

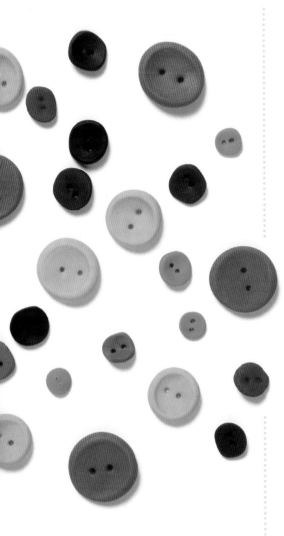

Soft-rimmed round buttons:

1. Pinch off a piece of polymer clay.

2. Roll a ball between the palms of your hands.

3. Use the pad of your right thumb to flatten the center of the ball in the center of your left palm to give a lovely smooth indent and a raised outer edge.

4. Poke 2 holes from the front with a skewer, then bake according to the manufacturer's instructions.

Flat, round buttons:

1. Pinch off a piece of polymer clay.

2. Roll a ball between the palms of your hands.

3. Flatten the ball with a rolling pin.

4. Poke 2 holes from the front with a skewer, then bake according to the manufacturer's instructions.

When her quilt was nearing completion, Judy needed something to tie together the settings of crockery and cutlery on her small tablecloth. As an initial focal point of the quilt, the flowers in the center cried out for more detail. Large bold red buttons were chosen as this focus and worked to counteract the softness of the cool color batiks. We didn't even attempt to buy these buttons!

The Champagne's Open, 40″ × 42$^{1}/_{2}$″, by Judy Stocks, Western Australia, 2005

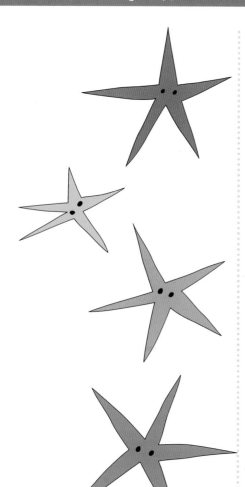

Star buttons became another finishing detail of Judy's quilt. The napkins spread around the table needed to be identified as such. Without unification, they would've been lost. Buttons tie in with the flowers, and, even better, a variety of colored star buttons adds spiky interest.

Star buttons:

1. Pinch off a piece of polymer clay.

2. Roll a ball between the palms of your hands.

3. Flatten the ball with a rolling pin.

4. Cut out a star shape, or any other shape you need, with a small craft blade. You may find that making a paper template and cutting around this works well for you.

5. Softly mold the edges of each star arm to round them a little.

6. Poke 2 holes from the front with a skewer, then bake according to the manufacturer's instructions.

Like an elephant balancing on a tiny ball or a seal balancing a ball on his nose, you should be feeling clever, energized, and thoroughly satisfied with yourself by now.

Settings

Of the many Magic Ballz made, most are treated simply and are stitched to square background blocks. These blocks are then stitched together, and a quilt is made. So far I've shown you ways to change the ballz themselves—but, wait, there's more!

By changing the placement of the ballz in the block and the blocks themselves, we can create very different-looking quilts.

BLOCK SHAPE AND PROPORTION

Let's get the ballz rolling along slowly with changes in settings. An easy place to start is to change where the ball is placed in the block. It doesn't have to be centered. The next change is the proportion of ball size to block size. The ball can float in a large background space or, it can squeeze into a small block. Finally, the block itself doesn't have to be square. A rectangle is still easy to piece in rows or columns but will vary the look considerably. This next sample illustrates all three changes.

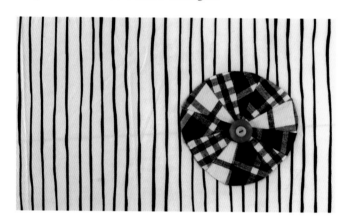

PIECED BACKGROUNDS

Many of us love piecing above all else. Your ballz could be normal and quickly made, then flung over a pieced background. A set of ballz could be made to enliven a boring UFO. Consider it part of the tradition of patchwork—making good from old.

Breaking the background into smaller squares is a good start.

Taking things further, the background could be broken into any pieced block—traditional, crazy, or contemporary. Assorted patchwork blocks could be pieced together to tell a story under the balls.

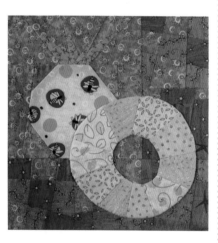

THINKING OUTSIDE THE BLOCK

No piecing. Wholecloth tops can be another way to approach ball placement. Sometimes just one fabric is all you need to link the ballz, and the only reason to break this fabric into background blocks would be for ease of appliqué. I did this on *Woolly Ballz* (page 75), where divisions aided the design and the execution of the appliqué. Sue, Judy, and Jeanne felt the look of their quilts would have been compromised if broken into blocks. Their quilts were still comparatively easy to appliqué in one piece.

  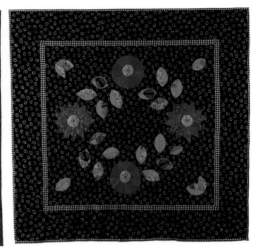

Lightly pieced. Tops can also be lightly pieced before placing ballz. Tracey stitched the wallpaper to the tablecloth before setting her platter of cupcakes in an appetizing position.

Sometimes just one fabric is all you need to link the ballz . . .

Traditional settings. Again, think back to traditional quilt settings. Look at placing the Magic Ballz in rows, in columns, as medallions, or in any way that fabrics can be joined to form a body.

 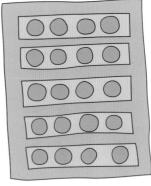 

Sparse placement. Change the usual proportion and make the Magic Ballz a small detail. This is a very contemporary look that works well in a minimalist interior, especially if made in low-contrast fabrics.

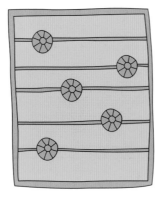  

Heavy placement. Place them very close together for a modern Magic Yo-Yo quilt. I think I would place the ballz on a background for strength.

Loose ballz. Scatter ballz over block divisions and borders. This can be subtle, like my few escapees in *Looking for My Prince* (page 68), which slightly blurred the block divisions. Or the ballz can be freely scattered with artful abandon.

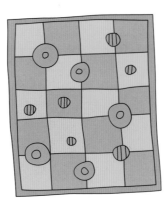 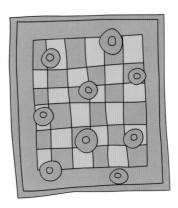

Does it have to be a quilt? Ballz can be let loose on absolutely anything. Bags, decorator pillows, clothing, book covers, pincushions, napkins, you name it.

Long Cuppa Cushion, 12½″ × 23″, by Christine Thompson, Western Australia, 2005

Magic Bag, 14″ × 8″, by Cindy Taylor, Western Australia, 2005

MAGIC BORDERZ

Most quilts need a border to frame the blocks, to unite the fabric scheme, or to highlight focus details. Magic Ballz can be used in borders in numerous ways. For starters, they can carry on the Magic Ballz theme in the quilt body, perhaps using smaller ballz or half ballz.

Borders with ballz. I particularly like the idea of making a very simply pieced or wholecloth body and placing the ballz in the border only. Place them sparsely or densely. Cut them in half and appliqué them in place. Back and stitch them on the quilt edge. The choice is yours.

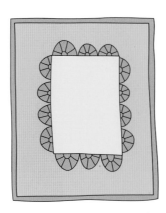

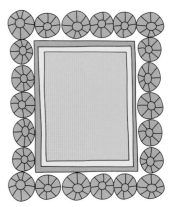

If you like making shapes other than ballz, the options increase yet again.

Think about the variations and possibilities . . .

Snakes, not ballz. Unwind the shape of the foundation, turning Magic Ballz into snakes that run the length of the border. Long curvy shapes can be difficult to piece in borders. Add a multitude of fabrics into the equation, and most of us would give up on the idea pretty quickly. A wedge-filled border appliquéd to your quilt would be a good resolution.

For ease of design, estimate the space that needs filling and roughly cut the foundation to fit. Quickly mark a sweet line by freehand, then refine the curves as you cut. How you cover the foundations is arbitrary—strips, wedgez, crazy.

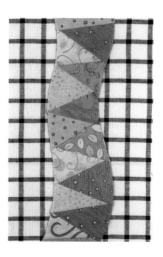

Wedge borders. I used up excess wedgez and balanced color and design on two quilts, *Predictions of a Colorful Future* (page 64) and *Looking for My Prince* (page 68). Working on a paper foundation reduces bulk; the paper also gives the wedgez a stable, easy-to-trim base.

Magic Endingz

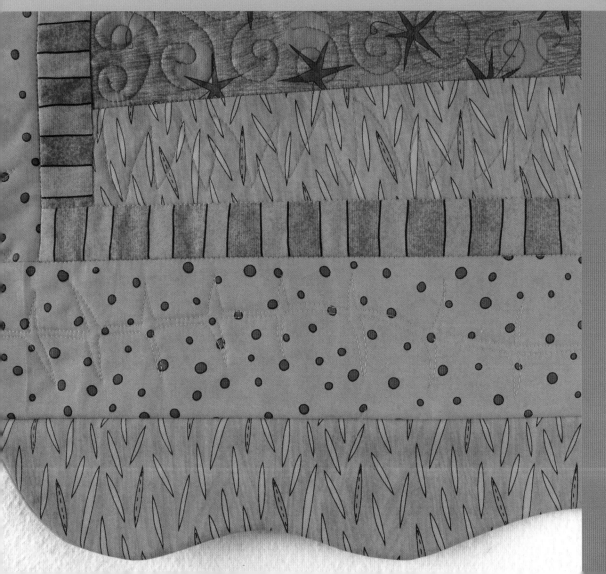

We're getting close to our final goal, and the options left for individualizing your quilt are diminishing. The top is complete, but there are still a multitude of finishing details to consider. I have finished my sample quilts in a variety of ways, not always the usual "sandwich, quilt, bind" method of traditional quiltmaking. Each time I deviated though, it was to make a better-looking quilt or to make the project easier.

BACKING

My backings are rarely one fabric. Often I piece fabrics left over from the quilt top. Sometimes, leftover blocks or borders are pieced in—not only to use them up but also to make a back that has more interest. Consider being creative or thrifty—whichever is your dominant character trait. Keep in mind that backing is technically just a "fabric" that is at least 1″ bigger than the quilt top on all sides.

SANDWICHING AND PINNING

Care needs to be taken when sandwiching backing, batting, and quilt top. With freshly pressed and tidy components, start sandwiching by laying the backing right side down on the floor or on a table and sticking the edges down, about a fist apart, with masking tape. Don't stretch the fabric, but do keep it taut. Layer on the batting and then the top right side up. Check that borders and blocks lie straight. Pin out from the edges of the Magic Ballz. Pin a channel on both sides of any borders or sashings that need to be quilted in-the-ditch. I also pin the edges of the quilt with long quilter's pins to secure the edges before I staystitch the edge.

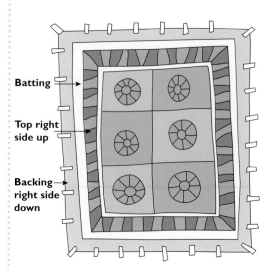

Batting
Top right side up
Backing right side down

QUILT WITH NO BINDING

The *Woolly Ballz* quilt (page 75) needed a different treatment. The top and backing were made as usual, but because they were thick and embroidered in a folk style, machine quilting wasn't an option. I also did not want binding. The solution was sandwiching to give solid edges, as I did when making the Magic Endingz.

Place batting on the floor. Layer the quilt top right side up and then the backing right side down. The top and backing must be the same size. The backing needs to be made from two pieces of fabric, with the seam left partially open so that you can turn out the quilt.

Pin the edges and stitch through all layers. Turn the quilt and press. Hand stitch the backing seam opening closed. Pin the sandwich as necessary and lightly hand stitch, button, or tie the quilt. A little machine quilting is possible, but too much will distort the quilt edge.

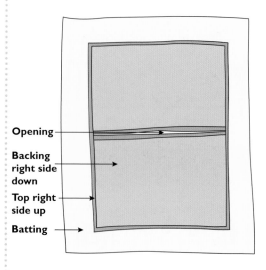

Opening
Backing right side down
Top right side up
Batting

QUILTING

My quilting is an integral part of my quiltmaking style. It is a part of the whole visual equation. My methods aren't complex, just a little different from the norm.

After sandwiching, I staystitch the edges held by the quilter's pins. To hold the sandwich together and to define the images, I stitch in-the-ditch around the Magic Ballz, borders, and blocks. I may also stitch in-the-ditch other details, like the center seam in a leaf. Where possible, stitch in-the-ditch with your walking foot on your machine.

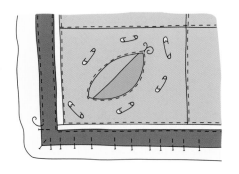

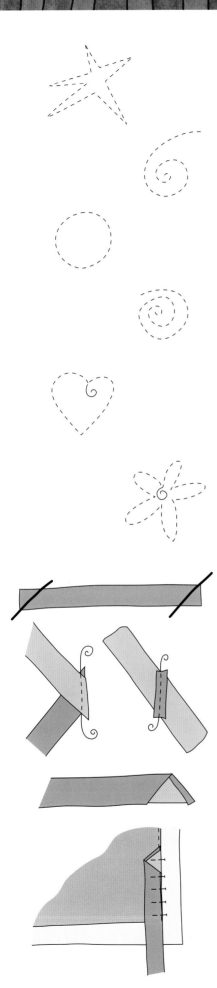

With feed dogs down, walking foot on, and a thread top and bottom that closely match the fabric, you are ready to quilt. I rarely continuous quilt, preferring instead to quilt small details that add texture or add to the quilt's story.

I don't mark my quilts. With many of my Magic Ballz projects, the quilting was simple. The motifs can be seen in the background of the project instructions. Most needed circular motifs in keeping with the established round theme.

HOW-TO:

1. Start and stop each image with about 6 tiny stitches and then slide the work to the next area. Fill spaces with imperfect shapes that the eye will meld beautifully.

2. Keep the stitching density similar across the quilt, otherwise the quilt may warp—more or denser stitching will pull the quilt sandwich closer together.

3. Finish by clipping the threads on top close to the stitching. Flip the quilt and clip the threads on the back.

BINDING

I've made lots and lots of quilts in my life, and 99 percent have been bound this way. It is a simple, firm binding that is the right size for all quilts.

HOW-TO:

1. Cut the required number of 2″ strips to go around the edge.

2. Cut each end of each strip at a 45° angle, with the right side of the fabric face up and aiming the cut up to the right.

3. To join the pieces, place them right sides together, points poking, allowing for the 1/4″ seam. Stitch and press the seams open.

4. Fold the binding in half lengthwise, wrong sides together. Press the starting angled edge under 1/4″, then fold and press the binding in half along the length, wrong sides together.

5. Start pinning the binding about 1/3 of the way across the bottom edge, starting with the pressed end and working in a clockwise direction. Pin the first side, making sure to line up the raw edges of the binding with the raw edges of the quilt top. Pin at 2″ intervals, frequently checking that the quilt lies flat and true. Place the last pin 1/4″ in from the first corner.

6. Use a walking foot to stitch a 1/4″ seam along this first side from the start of the binding to the corner. Stop with a backstitch at the last pin. Remove the quilt from the machine to miter the corner.

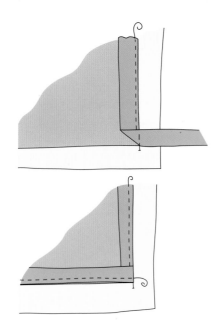

7. Lay the quilt on the table and fold the binding backward at the first corner at a 45° angle. Place a pin along the outer raw edge of the binding to hold the binding back at that angle. Fold the binding back along the next edge.

8. Pin along the next side at 2″ intervals, as before. Miter the next corner and proceed in the same manner until you are back to the first and final side.

9. Trim off the finishing end of the binding so that it fits snugly into the starting piece of the binding. Do this at an echoing 45° angle. Pin and stitch this final side.

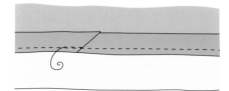 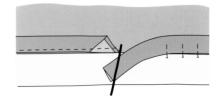

10. Trim off all the extra batting and backing so it is level with the raw edges of the binding.

11. Fold the binding to the back and pin in place.

12. Hand stitch the fold of the binding to the stitching you have just completed. The appliqué stitch also functions well here. Fold and tuck in the excess at each corner to echo the miter on the front. I find it best to stitch in a clockwise direction to form a neater miter.

MAGIC ENDINGZ AND THEIR SPECIAL BACK BINDING

I started by placing Magic Edgez under the edges of the Magic Ballz before they were stitched down. I continued with Magic Centerz, which have a turning at the back that becomes hidden once it is stitched in position on the Magic Ballz. I concluded with Magic Endingz—shaped sandwiches that edge the quilt. All work the same way but require slightly different considerations. The problem with Magic Endingz is that a traditional binding just doesn't work. A new method is essential if the top is quilted as usual. I call it *back binding* for want of a better description.

Make your Magic Endingz sandwiches in one of the following styles. Each sandwich consists of a lightweight batting, top fabric right side up, and backing fabric right side down. Size and shape are up to you, but in general, you should allow 1/2″ at the opening edge for trimming and seam allowance and 1/8″ (which is essentially next to nothing) for other seam allowances. I mark the shapes roughly and pin lightly, then try for sweet, yet varied shapes at the machine. Use a walking foot and a knee lift, if you have them, to make the job much easier! A smaller stitch than usual is insurance for easy turning.

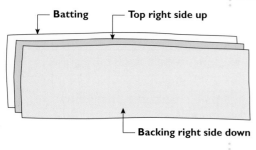

Batting   Top right side up

Backing right side down

Singles. These have an open end and are usually cut from a rectangle.

 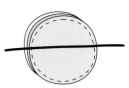

Pairs. These include a shape enclosed by stitches then sliced apart, usually across the center, to create two singles.

Rows. Economy of time and fabric rule here! Work in one direction or top and tail individual shapes. Stitching can be continuous. A couple of stitches at the base of each shape can be cut through or trimmed off.

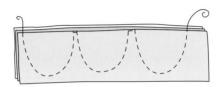 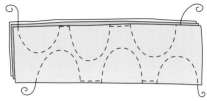

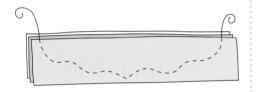

Whole. This strip sandwich that has one side open and one side stitched works especially well on pillows.

Trim 1/8˝ out from the stitching, clipping any valleys and points up to the stitching. Turn right side out. Press. Trim lower edge.

Top fabrics can be pieced, too!

Place your completed Magic Endingz on your quilt top, aligned with the quilt's raw edge. Pin in place. You may also choose to staystitch.

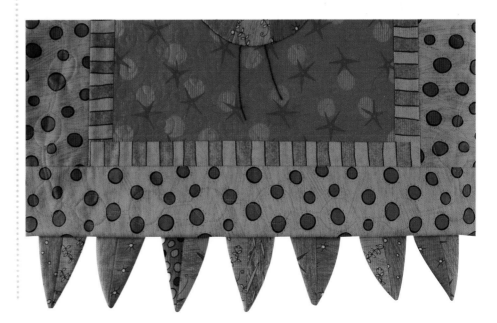

SPECIAL BACK BINDING

HOW-TO

2.

3.

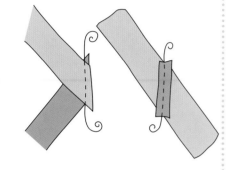

4.

1. Cut the required number of 2″ strips to cover the edge.

2. Cut each end of each strip at a 45° angle, with right sides up and aiming the cut up to the right.

3. To join the pieces, place them right sides together, points poking, allowing for the 1/4″ seam. Stitch and press the seams open.

4. Trim the start edge straight and press under 1/4″. Fold in half lengthwise, wrong sides together. Press.

5. Start along any side and pin the binding right side down on the top and Magic Endingz, with all raw edges aligned. Pin to the first corner, with the last pin sitting 1/4″ in from the edge.

6. Use a walking foot to stitch a 1/4″ seam from the start of the binding to the corner. Stop with a backstitch at the last pin, 1/4″ in from the corner. Remove the quilt from the machine to miter the corner.

7. Lay the quilt on the table and fold the binding backward at the first corner at a 45° angle. Place a pin level with the stitching line to hold the binding. Clip from the stitching to the corner. Fold the binding back along the next edge.

8. Pin along the next side at 2″ intervals. Start stitching 1/4″ in from the edge. Join up with previous stitching.

9. Continue around the edge, mitering the corners until you are back to the first and final side. Trim off the finishing end of the binding so that it fits snugly into the starting piece of the binding. Do this at an echoing 45° angle. Pin and stitch this final side.

10. Trim the corners. Pull the binding to the back and pin. Use a running stitch to hold down the edge.

Ta da! Scored a nice ending here, eh?

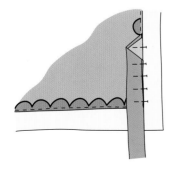

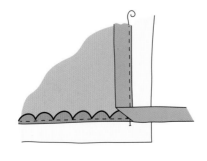

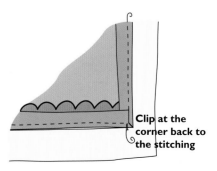

Clip at the corner back to the stitching

CHAPTER 9

Making Magic

The aim of the projects in a technical book such as this is to integrate the techniques into a workable item, giving you an opportunity to put theory into practice. When I design a project, I often start with a finished image in my mind and go about trying to complete something like that image in an easy-to-make manner.

In combining different processes in these projects, I aim to give you work order and technical capability so that you can make the project. I also want to show you how I have solved problems and altered my normal methods on the way toward developing that image. Even if you don't make these projects, just reading through them may open a new way of thinking or help you solve problems in the future.

Some of these projects made me change my mind about what I enjoy doing. Many stretched my thinking, and most, at the very least, combined techniques. Only the first project, Predictions of a Colorful Future (page 64), can be seen as a "normal" Magic Ballz quilt.

I'm tossing the ballz to you now . . . HEADZ UP!

Predictions of a Colorful Future

Predictions of a Colorful Future, Jan Mullen, 57″ × 57″, 1998

Making this, my third Magic Ballz quilt, was both an exploration of the familiar and a small step forward. I remember having the luxury of time to make a quilt without a deadline and how I enjoyed using color in a different way from the previous two Magic Ballz quilts, which were both quickly made specifically as class samples.

The difference from the past samples? Each ball celebrates one color instead of having the same fabrics repeated in each. The tone-on-tone wedgez of each ball are spiced up with an unpredictable choice. The sashing works to separate the blocks, while uniting these distantly related colored ballz. To finish, the extra wedgez in the border nicely link both the sashings and the ballz. I still like it all these years later.

THE ESSENTIAL SUPPLIES

Foundation paper: 9 squares 10″ × 10″-ish each

Block backgrounds, centers, and inner border: 2½ yards assorted black prints

Wedgez, sashing, outer border, and binding: 4½ yards assorted colors (6″ cuts or scraps are economical.)

Backing: 3½ yards

Batting: 61″ × 61″

Appliqué thread to match fabric choices

Stitching/quilting thread: black

THE BACKGROUND

Cut 9 squares 14″ × 14″ from black fabrics.

THE MAGIC BALLZ

1. Freehand cut 9 circles from the 10″-ish squares of paper. Cut a center hole in each, 1″-ish in diameter. Cutting holez off-center is fine.

2. Cut 6″ strips of wedgez fabrics the length you require. Stack them in color piles of 5–6 fabrics and slice them into wedgez of varying sizes, top width 2″–4″-ish and bases 0–1″-ish. Don't cut too many to start with. I used approximately 14 wedgez per circle.

3. Stitch the wedgez to the foundation. Finish the ball with the machine closure or pin in preparation for hand appliqué. Trim the outer edge fabric excess to ¼″-ish.

4. Arrange the background blocks and pin the ballz in position. Appliqué ballz to the blocks by hand or machine.

5. From background fabrics, cut out 9 stars to cover the centerz. To avoid the "hollow" effect, use a fabric different from the block background. Appliqué by hand or machine.

THE SASHING

1. Cut a variety of squares 2½″ × 2½″ from wedgez fabric. Join groups of 7 in a row to make each sashing strip. You will need 24. As this measurement is too big for the block, trim each sashing trip to 14″—the reduction is hard to see.

2. Cut 16 squares 2½″ × 2½″ from background fabric. These "stops" join the sashing strips.

3. Arrange your blocks. Arrange sashing strips around the blocks to balance. Place the stops in position. Stitch into sashing/block rows and stop/sashing rows. Stitch together the resulting small and large rows.

THE BORDERS

1. From the inner border fabric, cut strips 1″ by length of the fabric. Stitch these together to make 2 side borders 1″ × 49″ and top and bottom borders 1″ × 50″. Stitch on the side borders, then the top and bottom borders.

2. If you want to miter the corners like I did, cut and join lengths of paper for the border foundation to make 4 borders 4″ × 58″. *If you prefer not to miter the corners, cut the side borders 4″ × 50″ and the top and bottom borders 4″ × 58″.*

3. Starting from the center of each side, stitch the wedgez to cover all of the paper. Overhang here will be cut off. You may like to balance the color for a rainbow effect or to work in a scrappier, freeform manner.

4. Trim the fabric to the size of the paper. Remove the paper. Pin, from the center out, along raw edges of quilt on all sides. Stitch. Stop and start seams ¼″ in from each corner. The corners of all 4 seams should just meet.

Work a corner at a time at the ironing board, with the quilt right side up. Fold back 1 border at a 45° angle, aligning the outer edges with the excess of the adjacent border. Press the fold. Carefully pull back and pin underneath on this fold. Stitch from the seam to the outer edge.

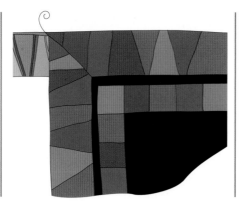

FINISHING

Sandwich and quilt, then bind and label. I machine quilted in-the-ditch of the starz, the ballz, the blocks, and the borders. Then I freemotion quilted small stars, kisses, and curls in the background of the blocks to make the ballz more prominent.

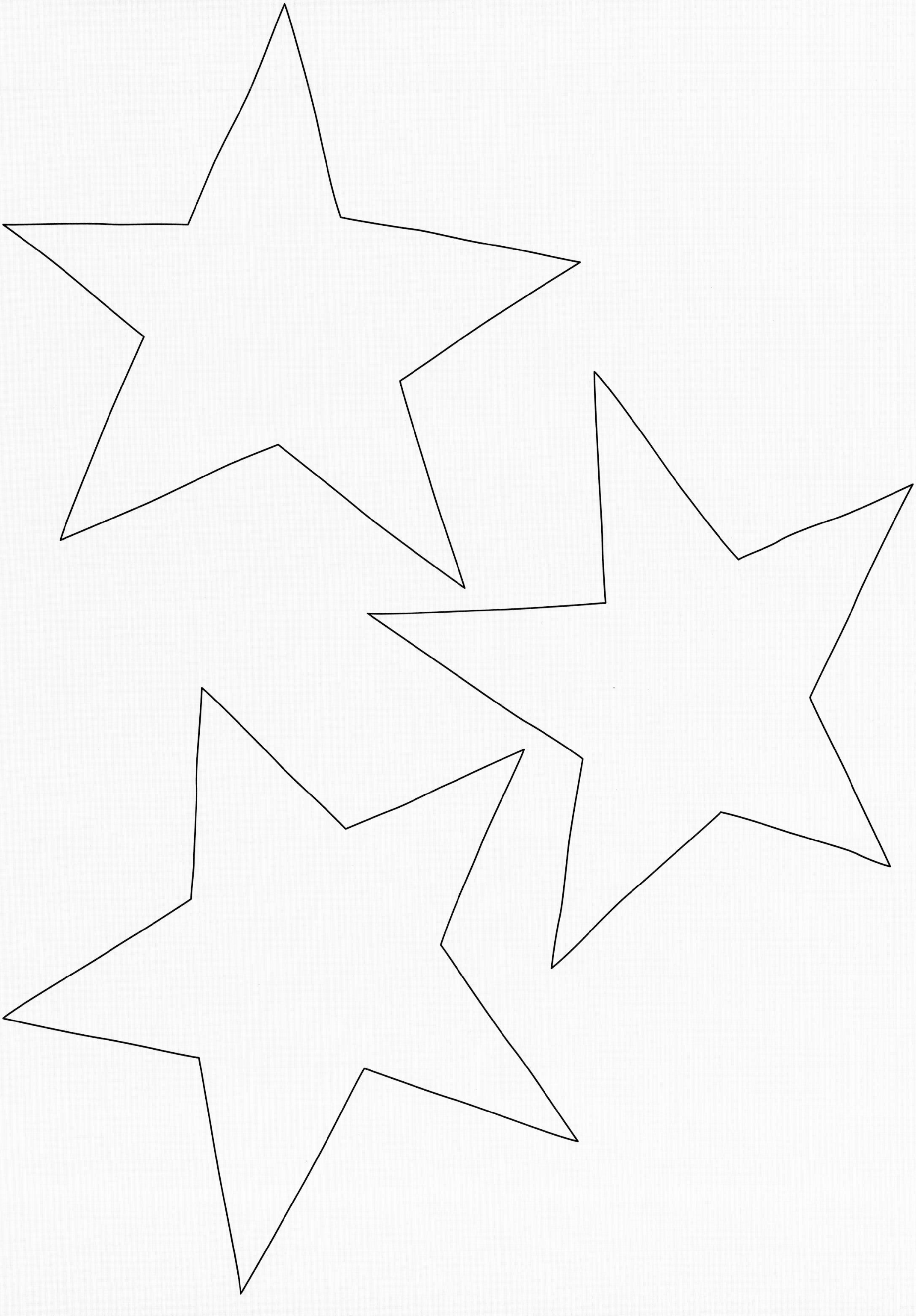

Looking for My Prince

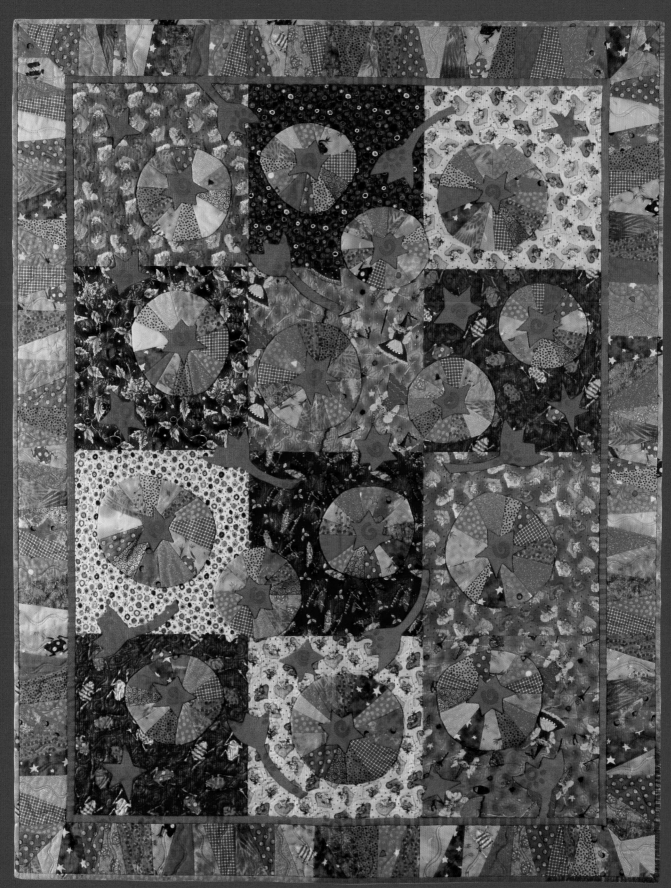

Looking for My Prince, Jan Mullen, 44$^{1}/_{2}$″ × 56$^{1}/_{2}$″, 1999

As has often happened with quilts, this, my fourth Magic Ballz, was prompted by the purchase of some interesting fabrics. These great frog fabrics hopped off the shelf and prompted me to change the way I worked. The Magic Ballz became a flotilla of lily pads. Then the lily pads needed more dimension, which resulted in a change of foundation from paper to batting that would not be removed. I had a new, more pleasant foundation, which has since become the springboard for other changes. The starz from *Predictions of a Colorful Future* (page 64) became lily flowers, and the extra pink silhouette flower shapes aided this visual suggestion.

This quilt was a breeze to make. I simply cut the backgrounds from squares of frog print fabrics. I then appliquéd a lily pad to each square before I pieced the top. I stitched extra lily pads and flowers between blocks. Finally, I pieced the border on paper from leftover lily pad edges.

THE ESSENTIAL SUPPLIES

Foundation: stabilized cotton batting to total 24″ × 40″

Assorted green fabrics: 3¼ yards total lily fabric for Magic Ballz, border, and binding

Pink print: ¾ yard for lily flowers, stars, and inner border

Frog fabric: 1¾ yards

Backing: 2¾ yards

Batting: 47″ × 59″

Appliqué thread: green and pink

Stitching/quilting thread to match fabric choices

THE BACKGROUND

Cut 12 squares 12½″ × 12½″-ish from frog fabric. Arrange and label them in finished order.

THE MAGIC BALLZ

1. Freehand cut 15 circles from batting squares varying in size from 5½″ × 5½″-ish to 7½″ × 7½″-ish. Each block has 1 circle/lily pad, with 3 extra to float between the blocks.
2. Cut a center hole in each, 1″-ish in diameter. Cutting holez off-center is good.
3. Cut strips of green lily pad fabrics 4½″ wide by the length you require. I started with a 4½″ × 12″ strip from each fabric. Stack them and slice into wedgez of varying sizes, with a maximum top width of 4″-ish. Don't cut too many to start with.
4. Stitch the wedgez to the foundation. Finish the ball with the machine closure or pin in preparation for hand appliqué. Trim the outer overhang fabric excess to a generous ¼″.

5. Arrange and pin a lily pad onto each background block. Don't center too many; move them around the blocks. For the extra lily pads that cross the blocks, mark their position with a safety pin and appliqué them later.
6. Appliqué the first 12 lily pads to the background blocks by hand or machine.
7. Stitch the blocks together.
8. Appliqué the extra blocks onto the quilt top.
9. Cut out 15 stars (renamed lilies here) to cover the centers. Cut out 9 free-floating lilies to cascade down the quilt. Cut extra, as needed, to fill any gaps. Appliqué on.

THE BORDERS

1. From the inner border fabric, cut strips 1″ by the width of the fabric. Piece together to make 2 side borders 1″ × 48½″ and top and bottom borders 1″ × 37½″. Stitch on the side borders, then the top and bottom borders.

2. Cut and join lengths of paper for the border foundation to make 2 side borders 4″ × 59″ and top and bottom borders 4″ × 47″.

3. Starting from the center, stitch the wedgez to cover all of the paper.

4. Trim the fabric to the size of the paper, then remove the paper.

5. Pin each of the 4 sides from the center out. Stitch, stopping and starting the seams 1/4″ in from each corner. The seams should just meet at the corners. Work on a corner at a time at the ironing board, with the quilt right side up. Fold back 1 border at a 45° angle, aligning the outer edges with excess outer edges of the other border. Press the fold. Carefully fold back and pin underneath on this fold. Stitch from the seam to the outer edge.

THE FINISHING

Sandwich and quilt, then bind and label. My machine quilting was quite simple: Lots of curls and double stars helped push back the backgrounds after I stitched in-the-ditch around the ballz and flowers. The borders were well-held with wobbly lines in the center of every wedge.

I See Spotz

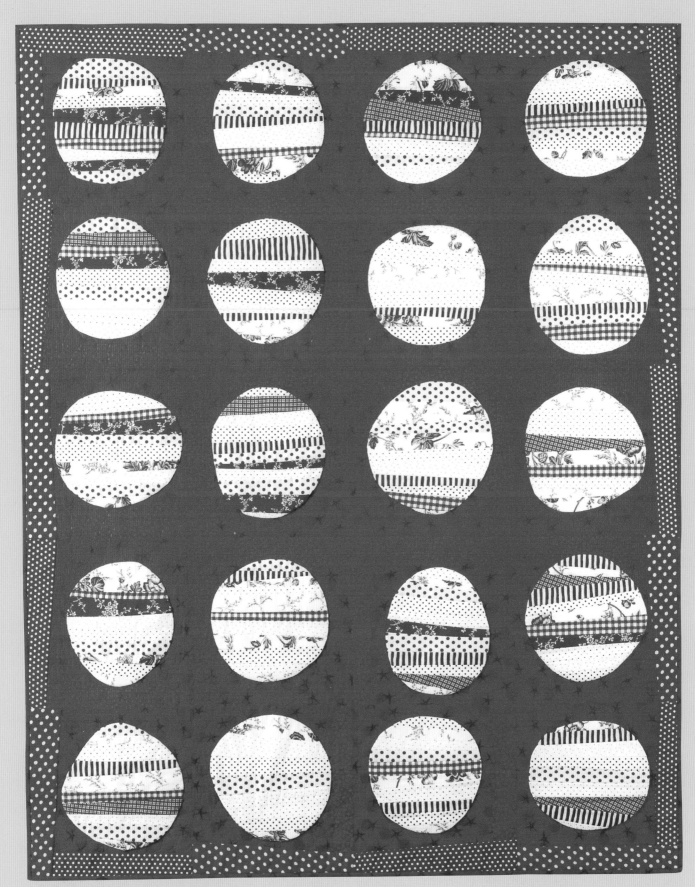

I See Spotz, Jan Mullen, 52″ × 65″, 2005

A small picture of an old quilt and a collection of red and white fabrics prompted a quick quilt that I couldn't resist making. These Magic Ballz have no centers but are still made in the normal ballz size. The foundation is covered by strips sewn vertically rather than wedgez.

The block backgrounds have subtle detail. I started with squares of only one background fabric and perked up areas by giving each block borders on two sides. Those with prominent spots were arranged to form a self-made outer border, while a subtler fabric divided the blocks internally.

Simple, graphic, and spotty, is this a perfect teenage quilt or what?

THE ESSENTIAL SUPPLIES

Foundation: stabilized cotton batting to total 50″ × 40″ or 20 squares each 10″ × 10″

Red tone-on-tone (red on red) fabric: 3 yards total for backgrounds and binding

Second red tone-on-tone (red on red) fabric: 1 yard for first block borders

Red and white (white on red) fabric: ½ yard each of 2 fabrics for the second and third block borders

White and red (red on white) fabric: 10 fat quarters for the Magic Ballz strips

Backing: 3¼ yards

Batting: 56″ × 63″

Appliqué thread: off-white

Stitching/quilting thread: red

THE BACKGROUND

1. Cut 20 squares 12½″ × 12½″-ish from background fabric.
2. Cut 16 rectangles 3″ × 13″-ish from the first block border fabric. Cut 2 rectangles 3″ × 13″-ish from the second block border fabric. Cut 2 rectangles 3″ × 13″-ish from the third block border fabric.
3. Stitch each rectangle to a background square. Lightly trim an adjacent side, skewing the slice to either the left or the right to straighten the edge and change the shape.

4. Cut 6 rectangles 3″ × 15″-ish from the first block border fabric. Stitch each to the trimmed edge of a first-bordered block.

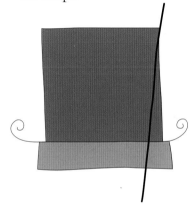

5. Cut 7 rectangles 3″ × 15″-ish from the second block border fabric. Stitch 1 to the trimmed edge of 5 first-bordered blocks. Stitch 1 to the trimmed edge of 2 second-bordered blocks.

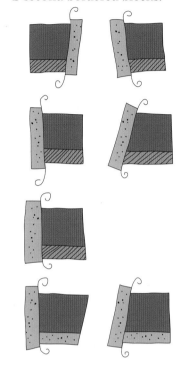

6. Cut 7 rectangles 3″ × 15″-ish from the third block border fabric. Stitch 1 to the trimmed edge of 5 first-bordered blocks. Stitch 1 to the trimmed edge of 2 third-bordered blocks.

7. Trim the blocks to
13½″ × 13½″. Crooked is good.

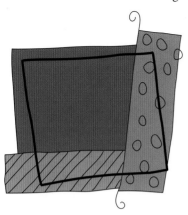

THE MAGIC BALLZ

1. Cut 20 circles, freehand and
funky, from 10″ × 10″-ish squares
of batting.

2. Cut strips from your Magic Ballz
fabric along the lengthwise
grain. Taper them from 3″-ish to
1″-ish. Don't cut too many to
start with. Cutting them to size
as needed will help balance the
size and color of the ballz.

3. Stitch the strips to the foundation, leaving about ½″ overhang
and alternating the direction of
the taper. If you start in the center,
you can soon stitch on both
edges and use up smaller fabrics.

4. Trim the excess outer edge fabric
to a generous ¼″.

THE FINISHING

1. Arrange the blocks in a pleasing
balance with the second and
third border fabrics, creating an
outer border. Pin on the Magic
Ballz and label the blocks in
finished order. Appliqué by hand
or machine.

2. Stitch the blocks together.

3. Sandwich and quilt, then bind
and label. I stitched in-the-ditch
the outer borders and ballz, then
lightly quilted circles in the
background squares.

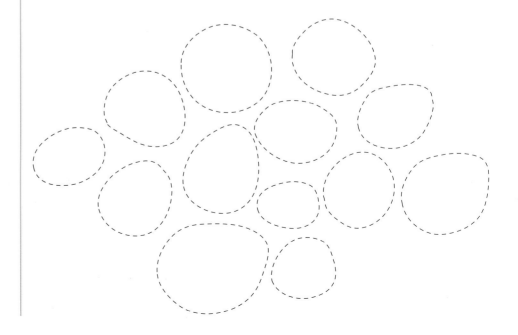

Woolly Ballz

Woolly Ballz, Jan Mullen, 52″ × 66¹/₂″, 2005

I hadn't made a wool quilt for a while. In years past, I've given myself an annual winter treat by making one wool quilt to add variety to my stitching life. The nature of thick woolen fabrics requires different thinking. Processes that are taken for granted when working with patchwork cottons may need to be reassessed. It's almost like taking a vacation!

Here I used the wool's "felting" ability to produce easy spiked Magic Ballz. The fabric went into the washing machine and under the steam iron before it was cut. No delicate treatment. The spikes could then remain raw-edged and be held by simple machine stitching. Hand-stitched embroidery in a variety of stitches added folksy details. The result is a sturdy, cuddly, primitive-style quilt.

THE ESSENTIAL SUPPLIES

Foundation paper: 12 squares 9″ × 9″-ish

Red wool fabrics: 3½ yards total for background and border (Requirements allow for preshrunk wool. *Allow more for shrinkage.*) Machine wash or steam iron before cutting. Width of wool fabrics vary. I have allowed for 40″ as a generic width.

Assorted wool fabrics: 12 fat quarters total for Magic Ballz, centers, and inner circles

Black wool fabric: ¼ yard for inner border

Backing: 1¾ yards each of 2 wool fabrics

Batting: 56″ × 72″

Stitching/appliqué thread to match the Magic Ballz fabrics

Black embroidery floss for hand stitching detail on and around the Magic Ballz

Red wool yarn for tying

THE BACKGROUND

Cut 12 squares 15″ × 15″-ish from background fabric.

THE MAGIC BALLZ

1. Freehand cut 12 circles from the paper foundation. Cut a center hole in each, 1″-ish in diameter. Cutting holez off-center is fine.
2. Cut strips of wedgez fabrics 7″-ish high by the length you require. Stack them and slice into wedgez of varying sizes, with a maximum top width of 4″ and with bases from 0 to 1″. Don't cut too many to start with.
3. Stitch the wedgez to the foundation, leaving a large overhang. Stitch only to the edge of the paper. Because I alternated colors, I had to plan wedge sizes in the final quadrant to keep the pattern. Finish the ball with the pieced closure (page 17).
4. Tear the paper foundation from the fabric. Trim back the outer edge fabric from the center to the seams. Don't worry about symmetry and beautifully neat edges.

5. Arrange and pin the ballz to the background blocks. Appliqué by hand or machine. I machine stitched down each wedge in-the-ditch, from the center to

the edge, before stitching ⅛″ in from the edge. I used a larger-than-normal stitch, which worked well visually with the thickness of the wool.

6. Cut 12 centers from 2″ × 2″-ish squares and 12 inner circles from 1″ × 1″-ish squares. Pin a pair of centers and circles over each hole. Appliqué by hand or machine.
7. Using 6 strands of embroidery floss, stitch out from the outer edges of each of the Magic Ballz with a large running stitch. Decoratively stitch the centers with either fly, cross, or stab stitch. Finish the inner circles with running stitch.

8. Trim the blocks to
14½″ × 14½″. Arrange the
blocks to balance. Stitch
together. I pressed the seams
open to keep the quilt flat.

THE BORDERS

1. From the inner border fabric,
cut strips 1″ by the width of the
fabric. Piece together 2 side
borders 1″ × 58½″ and top and
bottom borders 1″ × 44½″. Stitch
on the side borders, the top, and
the bottom.

2. From the outer border fabric,
cut strips by the length of the
fabric. Cut 2 strips 4″ × 59½″
and a top and bottom 4″ × 51½″.
Stitch on the sides, the top, and
the bottom.

THE BACKING

1. The backing should be the same
size as the top. Trim each piece
to 33¾″ × 51½″. Join the 2
pieces of backing along their
lengths, leaving the seam open in
the middle for about 20″. Press
the entire seam allowance open.

2. Sandwich the batting, the top
(right side up), and the backing
(wrong side up), aligning the
edges of the top and backing.
Stitch a ¼″ seam around these
edges. Trim the batting level
with the other edges. Clip across
the corners. Turn the quilt right
side out. Close the opening with
hand stitches—either invisible
or decorative.

THE FINISHING

1. I lightly pinned the quilt and
machine quilted in-the-ditch
around the ballz, blocks, and
inner borders. Doing so, crisply
defined these areas and held the
sandwich together.

2. I used wool yarn to tie the quilt
together and to introduce
another folksy textural aspect.
To avoid migrating fibers, I
suggest using an old wool blanket
as batting if you want to tie with
wool. Label the quilt.

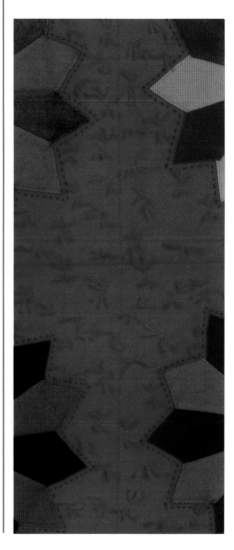

Maximum Magic

Maximum Magic, Jan Mullen, 36$\frac{1}{2}$″ × 44$\frac{1}{2}$″, 2005

I had the fabrics. I knew I wanted Magic Edgez and Magic Endingz. I thought crib-quilt sized would be appropriate for my fanciful thoughts. Still, this project evolved very slowly. So different was this in style from my usual quilts that I continually stopped to assess that I was on the right track. Even now, I love it but still wonder where it came from!

The final quilt features small ballz with yo-yo centers and Magic Edgez that were machine-stitched onto a very simple alternating-squares background. Interestingly, I quilted the top before stitching on the ballz—a different approach. The final Magic Endingz are held in place with a binding that isn't seen from the front—my special back binding.

THE ESSENTIAL SUPPLIES

Foundation: stabilized cotton batting to total 12″ × 16″

Violet fabric #1: 1¼ yards for backgrounds, border, and back binding

Violet fabric #2: ¾ yard for alternate backgrounds

2 plaid fabrics: a fat quarter each for wedgez

Plaid fabric: ½ yard for second inner border and wedgez

Hot pink solid fabric: ⅓ yard for first inner border and yo-yos

Green solid fabric: 1 yard for ballz backings, Magic Edgez, and Magic Endingz

Batting: 40″ × 48″

Lightweight foundation (Pellon): 10″ × 40″ for Magic Edgez and Magic Endingz

Backing: 1¼ yards

Appliqué thread: green and pink

Stitching/quilting thread to match fabric choices

THE BACKGROUND

1. Cut 20 squares 8½″ × 8½″-ish from background fabrics. Arrange in an alternating set. Stitch together.
2. From the first border fabric, cut strips 1″ by the width of the fabric. Piece together to make 2 side borders 1″ × 40½″ and top and bottom borders 1″ × 33½″. Stitch on the side borders, then the top and the bottom borders.
3. From the second border fabric, cut 1″ strips across the bias of the fabric. Piece together to make 2 side borders 1″ × 41½″and top and bottom borders 1″ × 34½″. Stitch on the side borders, then the top and bottom borders. To ease the drag, stitch with the plaid bias fabric on the bottom.
4. From the third border fabric, cut strips 1¾″ by the width of the fabric. Piece together 2 side borders 1¾″ × 42½″ and top and bottom borders 1¾″ × 37″. Stitch on the side borders, then the top and bottom

borders, again with the bias plaid fabric underneath.
5. Sandwich and quilt. I machine quilted freehand diagonal grids on one fabric and curls on the other.

THE MAGIC BALLZ

1. Cut 12 squares 4″ × 4″-ish from batting. Cut freehand circles from these. Cut a center hole in each, 1″-ish in diameter. Cutting holez off-center is fine.
2. Cut strips of plaid fabrics 3″-ish high by the length you require. Stack and slice them into wedgez of varying sizes, with a maximum top width of 2″ and bases between 0 and 1″-ish. Don't cut too many to start with. I used 9 wedgez per ball.
3. Stitch the wedgez to the foundation. Finish each ball with the machine closure (page 17). Cut squares 5″ × 5″-ish from violet fabrics #1 and #2. Place the ballz and backing right sides together. Stitch together, just out from the edge of the batting. Trim the fabric excess to ¼″. It may be possible to turn the Magic Ballz through the hole. If not, cut an opening cross in the backing and turn the Magic Ballz right side out (page 38). Press.

Use an invisible hemming stitch to machine appliqué the ballz and edgez to the quilt.

3. Cut 12 squares 3″ × 3″-ish from yo-yo fabric. Cut circles freehand, stitch the edges, and gather to form yo-yos (page 45). Appliqué by machine, using an invisible hemming stitch.

THE MAGIC ENDINGZ

1. Cut 4 strips of lightweight foundation 3″ × 20″-ish. Cut 8 strips of green solid fabric also 3″ × 20″-ish. You will need 72 petals, 18 from each strip. Mark freehand petals (page 40), with a base of 1½″ to 2″ and a gap of ¼″. Stitch. Trim to ⅛″ out from stitching. Turn each right side out, then press and trim the open ends.

2. Place the Magic Endingz around the edges of the quilt, with raw edges aligned with those of the quilt. Staystitch in position. Make a back binding (page 62). Stitch on the back binding. Press. Turn and hand stitch in place, mitering the corners. Bind and label.

THE MAGIC EDGEZ

1. Cut 4 strips of lightweight foundation 2″ × 20″-ish. Cut 8 strips of green solid fabric also 2″ × 20″-ish. Mark 72 petals freehand (page 40), with a base of 1½″ to 2″ and a gap of ¼″. Stitch. Trim to ⅛″ out from stitching. Turn each right side out, and then press and trim the open ends.

2. Arrange and pin Magic Ballz onto the background blocks. Place 6 Magic Edgez under each ball and hold them in place with 2 pins each (using only 1 pin allows them to move about).

Yellow Bloomz

Yellow Bloomz, Jan Mullen, 25$\frac{1}{2}$″ × 28$\frac{1}{2}$″, 2004

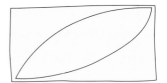

What started as a small class sample to encourage students to move on from the "normal" Magic Ballz concept has become a firm favorite among students. It serves well as an introduction to the technique and can successfully be made in a one-day class.

Changes are small. We first change the size of the ballz. We then move on to cutting shapes other than ballz and covering them with strips or rectangles. The centers of the flowers are then covered with free-cut yo-yos. It is a lovely sampler of techniques that is quick and easy to do and that can easily be expanded to make a larger quilt.

THE ESSENTIAL SUPPLIES

Foundation: stabilized cotton batting to total 20″ × 10″

Assorted blue fabrics: ⅞ yard total fabric for background, border, and binding

Assorted yellow fabrics: ⅓ yard for flowers, yo-yos, and inner border

Assorted green fabrics: small scraps for leavez

Assorted black-and-white fabrics: scraps to total ⅛ yard for the vase

Backing: 29″ × 32″

Batting: 29″ × 32″

Stitching/quilting/appliqué thread to match fabric choices

THE BACKGROUND

Cut background fabric 18″ × 21″.

THE FLOWERS

1. Cut 3 squares 5″ × 5″-ish from batting. Cut a freehand circle from each. Cut a center hole in each, 1″-ish in diameter. Cutting holez off-center is fine.

2. Cut strips of flower fabrics 3″-ish wide by the length you require. Stack them and then slice into wedgez of varying sizes, with a maximum top width of 2½″ and bases from 0 to 1″. I used 9 wedgez per ball.

3. Stitch the wedgez to the batting. Finish the ballz with the machine closure or pin in preparation for hand appliqué (page 19). Trim the overhang to a generous ¼″.

THE VASE

1. Cut a rectangle 7″ × 8″-ish from batting. Trim the rectangle to taper at the base.

2. Cut strips of vase fabrics 1½″ × 8″-ish. I used 6 strips. I cut my rim a little wider, at 2″ × 8″-ish.

3. Stitch the strips to the vase foundation, stopping just short of the top. Stitch the rim over the top edges of the vertical strips. Trim the outer edge fabric excess to a generous ¼″.

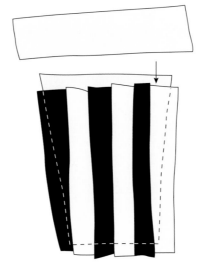

THE LEAVEZ

1. Cut 2 rectangles 2″ × 5″-ish from batting. Cut a leaf shape from each.

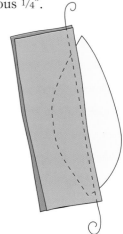

2. Cut 4 rectangles 2½″ × 5½″-ish from leaf fabrics.

3. Stitch the rectangles, right sides together, across the center of the leaf foundation. Trim the outer edge fabric excess to a generous ¼″.

ALL TOGETHER

1. Arrange and pin the flowers, vase, and leavez to the background. Appliqué by hand or machine.

2. From the inner border fabric, cut 2 side borders 1″ × 21″ and top and bottom borders 1″ × 19½″. Stitch on the side borders, then the top and bottom borders.

3. From the outer border fabric, cut and piece fabrics to make 2 side borders 3½″ × 22″ and top and bottom borders 3½″ × 25″. Stitch on the side borders, then the top and bottom borders.

4. Cut 3 squares 4″ × 4″-ish from yo-yo fabric. Stitch yo-yos (page 45). Appliqué the yo-yos to the quilt.

THE FINISHING

Sandwich and quilt, then bind and label. My machine quilting was simple. After stitching in-the-ditch, I covered the background with spirals and accentuated the borders with freehand lines.

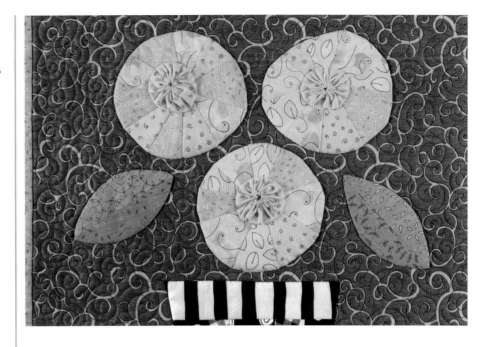

Grow Daizy Grow

Grow Daizy Grow, Jan Mullen, 20″ × 57″, 2005

My thumbnail sketches of "character" Magic Ballz—ballz with faces—have beckoned for years. In a moment of inspiration, I designed a garden full of happy flowers and smiling suns. Once I made one, I found it hard to stop.

Only the flower petals are something like the "normal" Magic Ballz. The center is a large piece of batting covered with one piece of fabric. The leavez and stalk are composed of two fabrics.

This height chart could easily be lengthened or shortened by cutting the background to suit its recipient or position on the wall. It has a striped fabric to help record the relevant names, dates, and heights in permanent marker or with embroidery. An alternative would be to stitch a tape measure alongside the border to make measuring easier and the quilt's function more obvious.

Try using this design for the center panel of a bed quilt. Join a few together to make a garden quilt. Tie it in with *The Birdz and the Beez* (page 87) when decorating a child's room.

THE ESSENTIAL SUPPLIES

Foundation: stabilized cotton batting to total 16″ × 45″

Teal fabric: 1¾ yards for the background and binding

Assorted green fabrics: ⅔ yard total for stalk and leavez

Pink fabrics: fat eighth total for petals (scraps are fine)

Yellow fabric: 8″ × 8″ for face

White striped fabric: 3″ × 57″ for the height recorder

Backing: 1¾ yards

Batting: 24″ × 61″

Appliqué thread: green, pink, yellow

Stitching/quilting thread: teal

Embroidery floss: 20″ black for mouth

Buttons: 2 medium-sized black for eyes

THE BACKGROUND

Cut the background fabric lengthwise and trim to *exactly* 20″ × 57″.

THE FOUNDATION

1. Freehand cut the petals, face, stalk, and leaf foundations from rectangles of batting:
   petals: 12″ × 11″
   face: 7″ × 7″
   stalk: 2″ × 45″ to 3½″ × 45″
   leavez: 10 squares 5″ × 5″ to 6″ × 6″, cut across the corners

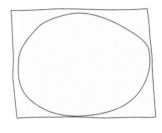
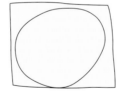

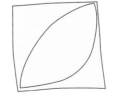

2. Cut a center hole 1″-ish in diameter in the petal foundation only.
3. Arrange all pieces on the background fabric to fine-tune the shapes.

THE DAISY

1. Cut individual petal fabrics 3″ × 6″-ish. Trim these down the sides to form wedgez with tops that are 3″-ish and bases that are 1″-ish. Pieces shorter than 6″ may also be used, as the center will be covered by the face. I used 14 wedgez.
2. Stitch the wedgez to the foundation. Finish the ball with the machine closure or pin in preparation for hand appliqué. Trim the overhang to a generous ¼″.
3. Cut the face fabric a generous ¼″ bigger than the foundation. Lightly pin in place, then lightly pin to the petals.

THE STALK

Cut the stalk fabric a generous ¼″ bigger than the foundation. To make the length, stitch smaller pieces to the stalk if desired. Lightly pin in place.

THE LEAVEZ

1. Cut 20 rectangles each 10″ × 4″-ish from leaf fabric. Pair the rectangles and place them right sides together, then place on their foundation with raw edges aligned near the center. Stitch. Being off-center at the points will make it easier to hand appliqué.
2. Trim the outer edge fabric excess to a generous ¼″.

ALL TOGETHER

1. Arrange all components in finished position on the background. Pin to hold. Appliqué by hand or machine.
2. Stitch on the button eyes.
3. Mark a mouth on the face. Using 3 strands of embroidery floss, backstitch over the marked line.

4. Stitch the height recorder fabric to the left or right side.

THE FINISHING

Sandwich and quilt, then bind and label. I machine quilted in-the-ditch around the foundations and the border. I filled the backgrounds with large circular curls. I also stitched in every stripe of the height recorder fabric to hold it well.

The Birdz and the Beez

The Birdz and the Beez, Jan Mullen, each 20˝ × 20˝ plus Magic Endingz, 2005

I loved making *Grow Daisy Grow* so much that I wanted to continue on in this vein. Lines from that old song, "… the birds and the bees and the flowers and the trees and the moon up above and a thing called love" popped into my head. Apologies to you for my terrible singing and to the original writer for my mangling of the lines, but the result of my warbling, I think, is worth it. Variations in foundation shape, wedgez shape, and Magic Endingz make this set of pillows fun to make and delightful to decorate with.

THE ESSENTIAL SUPPLIES

Foundation: stabilized cotton batting to total 20″ × 30″

Assorted fabrics: 5 yards total for Magic Ballz, backgrounds, and Magic Endingz

Inner border stripe: 1/2 yard total

Outer border fabrics: 1/4 yard for each pillow

Batting: 6 pieces each 22″ × 22″

Assorted fabrics: 6 pieces each 16″ × 41″ for pillow backs

Lightweight foundation (Pellon): 1 1/2 yards for Magic Endingz

Appliqué thread to match fabric choices

Stitching/quilting thread to match fabric choices

Buttons: pairs of black buttons for the bird, bee, flower, and moon

Embroidery floss: black for bee, flower and moon mouths, and bird legs

Decorator pillow forms: 6 each 20″ × 20″

THE PILLOW FRONTS

1. Cut 5 squares 12 1/2″ × 12 1/2″ from background fabric for the bird, bee, flower, tree, and heart pillows. Piece the moon background from 2 fabrics; cut the sky 13 1/2″ × 11 1/2″ and the grass 13 1/2″ × 3 1/2″. Stitch these pieces together and trim to 12 1/2″ × 12 1/2″.

2. Cut images from batting. You may like to draw them on 10″ × 10″ squares of paper first:
   bird: 10″ × 7″
   bee: bottom—3″ × 6″, tummy—2 1/2″ × 2″, head—2 1/2″ × 2″, wings—each 4″ × 2″
   flower: petals—5″ × 5″, face—3″ × 3″, leaves—each 5″ × 2″
   tree: 6″ × 8″, trunk—3/4″ × 3″
   moon: 7″ × 7″ (Cut a circle and take out a little circular bite!)
   heart: 8″ × 9″

3. Cut strips or wedgez of varying sizes to cover the foundation. All measurements are "ish":
   bird: various strips and wedgez in between the beak 2″ × 2″ and tail 4″ × 5″
   bee: bottom—8 strips, tapering from 1 1/2″ to 1″; tummy—3″ × 2 1/2″; head—3″ × 2 1/2″; wings—each 4 1/2″ × 2 1/2″
   flower: petals—10 wedgez, each cut from 2 1/2″ × 2 1/2″; face—3 1/2″ × 3 1/2″; leaves—4 rectangles each 5 1/2″ × 1 1/2″
   tree: 6 strips tapering from 1 1/2″ to 1″, treetop—3″ × 3″, trunk—cut from 1 piece 1 1/4″ × 3 1/2″

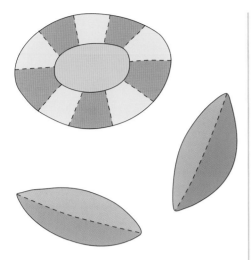

moon: cut from 1 piece 8″ × 8″

heart: 8 strips tapering from 1½″ to 1″

4. Stitch the various wedgez and strips to the foundation. Finish the flower using the machine closure. Trim the overhang to a generous ¼″ on all images.

5. Arrange and pin the images to the background blocks. Appliqué by hand or machine.

6. Stitch the eyes on the bird, bee, flower, and moon. I made my buttons from polymer clay (page 48).

7. Use a backstitch and 3 strands of embroidery floss to stitch the mouths on the bee, flower, and moon and the bird's legs, bee's antenna, and the flower stem.

THE BORDERS

1. Cut the inner border fabrics. For each decorator pillow, cut 2 side borders 1½″ × 12½″ and top and bottom borders 1½″ × 14½″. Stitch on the side borders, then the top and bottom borders.

2. Cut the outer border fabrics. For each decorator pillow, cut 2 side borders 3½″ × 14½″ and top and bottom borders 3½″ × 20½″. Stitch on the side borders, then the top and bottom borders.

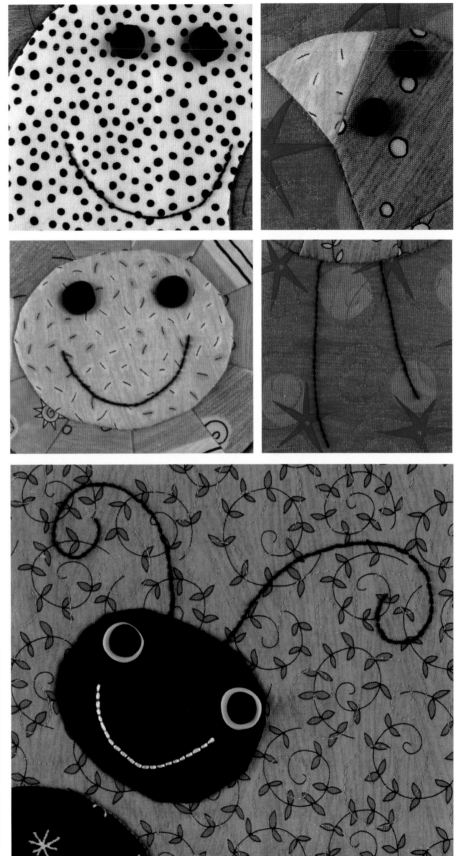

THE QUILTING AND THE MAGIC ENDINGZ

1. Sandwich the decorator pillow tops with batting, then quilt. After stitching in-the-ditch the inner borders and around the images, do some simple machine quilting, such as curls in the backgrounds and double line borders in the outer borders.

2. Make different Magic Endingz for each decorator pillow. Sandwiches refer to the light-weight foundation, top, and backing placed together. All measurements are a bit "ish." **bird:** Cut 28 rectangles of top fabrics 1½″ × 6½″. Piece these along their lengths. Cut 14 rectangles 2½″ × 6½″ from light-weight foundation and backing. Slice each stitched sandwich in half to make 28 wings for Magic Endingz.

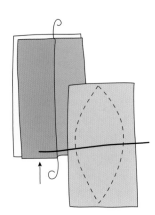

bee: Cut 4 strip sandwiches, each 3¼″ × 16″. Piece the top fabric from strips cut 1½″ × 16″, 1¼″ × 16″, and 1½″ × 16″. Cut 4 semicircles from each stitched sandwich strip for Magic Endingz.

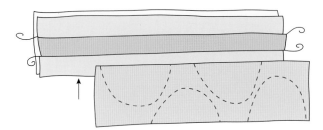

flower: Cut 12 rectangle sandwiches, each 3″ × 7″. Slice each stitched sandwich in half to make 24 leaves for Magic Endingz.

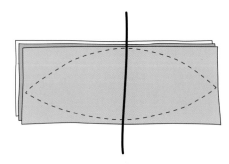

tree: Cut 5 strip sandwiches, each 2½″ × 17″. Cut 6 semicircles from each stitched sandwich strip for Magic Endingz.

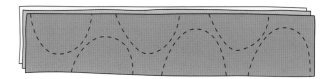

moon: Cut 4 rectangle sandwiches, each 3″ × 17″. Make 1 for each side for Magic Endingz.

heart: Cut 8 rectangle sandwiches, each 5″ × 6″. Slice each stitched sandwich in half to make 16 pieces for Magic Endingz.

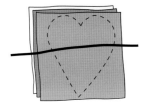

MAKING THE PILLOWS

1. For each pillow cut 2 pieces of backing 16″ x 20½″. Turn under ½″ on one long side of each piece. Press. Push the raw edge under again to meet the fold line. Press again. Stitch.

2. Place the quilted pillow front right side up. Place the Magic Endingz right side down on the pillow, with raw edges aligned.

3. Place both backs right side down on the front, creating a large overlap with the stitched edges at the center. Keep all raw edges level. Stitch a ¼″ seam all around. Trim the edges of the foundation level with the backs. Trim the corners. Turn the pillows right side out and ease in the pillow insert.

Boudoir Ballz

Boudoir Ballz, Jan Mullen,
14″ × 12″, 2004

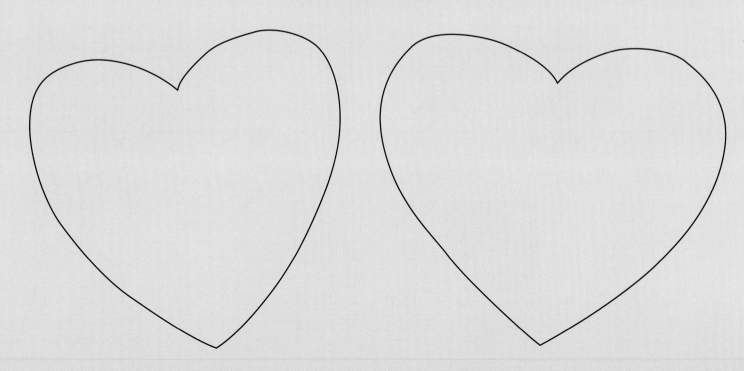

Throughout this book, I have had you thinking about placing your Magic Ballz on a background. Let's try a different approach: Why not make two ballz the same shape, forget the background, and do some stuffing? Result—pillow magic!

Flannel fabrics are a favorite of mine. They feel lovely, are great to cuddle, and are firm to stitch with. With flannel wedgez, a flannel heart center covering each hole, and a large pom-pom trim, you couldn't get much more touchy-feely! *Boudoir Ballz* made of slippery silks or satins with a lingerie lace edging could be a nice alternative. Ah, if only they suited my bedroom.

THE ESSENTIAL SUPPLIES

Foundation: stabilized cotton batting to total 12″ × 28″

Yellow flannel fabrics: fat eighth each of 4 prints for the pillow wedgez

Red flannel: 2 squares 5″ × 5″ for the heart centers

Pom-pom trim: 1 yard

Polyester fill: enough to suit

Appliqué thread: red

Stitching/quilting thread to match fabric choices

THE MAGIC BALLZ

1. Cut 2 pieces of batting, each 12″ × 14″. With both pieces together, freehand cut 2 circles, 1 for each side of the pillow. Cut a center hole in each, 1″-ish in diameter. The holez don't have to match.

2. Stack the flannel fabrics and slice them into wedgez of varying sizes, maximum top width 4″ and bases from 0 to 1″. I used 12 wedgez on each side.

3. Stitch the wedgez to the foundation. Leave at least 1/2″ overhang. Finish the ball using the machine closure. Trim the overhang to 1/2″.

4. Cut out 2 hearts to cover the centers. Appliqué by hand or machine.

THE PILLOW

1. Arrange and pin the pom-pom trim to the outer edge of the pillow front. Staystitch this if it is bulky. Pin the pillow back and front right sides together. Stitch together with a 1/2″ seam, leaving a 3″ opening for turning.

2. Turn the pillow right side out. Insert polyester fill. Stitch the opening closed by hand.

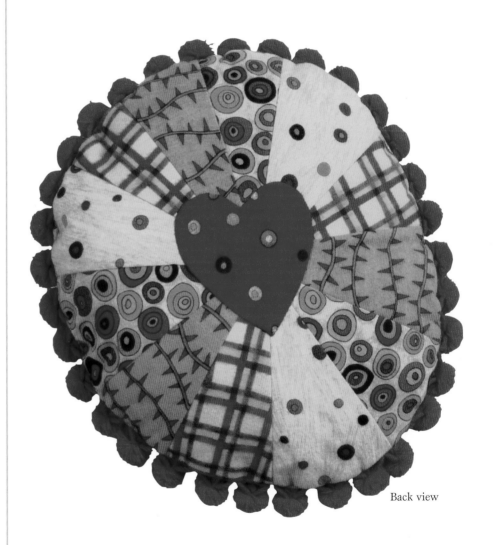

Back view

Who knows what the crystal ball holdz for the future?

About the Author

As a youngster, Jan Mullen's major ball interest lay with tennis and netballs. Years of working with fabric have narrowed her interest in balls to simply making representations of them.

Still, there are plenty of balls in her life. Husband Ben likes whacking golf balls. Sons Brodie and Keelan enjoy watching tough Aussie males kick their odd-shaped footballs. Daughter Miffy loves getting dressed up and going out to balls. Older dog Celeste spends much of her time curled up into a ball. Queen of Balls in the Mullen household, though, is younger dog Rocket, who has a never-ending and varied supply of balls stashed all over the house and yard.

Jan has a ball in her business life, too. As a designer under the business name Stargazey Quilts, she designs free and eazy contemporary quilt blocks. She complements this pattern business by designing fabrics for Marcus Brothers. Traveling the world, teaching others how to relax and be creative with stitch and fabric, completes the current picture of the author . . .

Jan Mullen
Stargazey Quilts
9-100 Stirling Highway
North Fremantle, Western Australia
Australia 6159
phone + 61 8 9433 3129
fax + 61 8 9433 3109
jan@stargazey.com
www.stargazey.com

Index

Great Titles

from 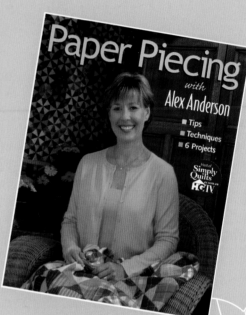 C&T PUBLISHING